THE NATIONAL STATUS
OF THE CHINESE IN INDONESIA
1900-1958

Donald E. Willmott

THE NATIONAL
STATUS OF THE
CHINESE IN INDONESIA
1900-1958

EQUINOX
PUBLISHING
JAKARTA KUALA LUMPUR

EQUINOX PUBLISHING (ASIA) PTE LTD
No 3. Shenton Way
#10-05 Shenton House
Singapore 068805

www.EquinoxPublishing.com

The National Status of the Chinese in Indonesia 1900-1958
by Donald E. Willmott

ISBN 978-602-8397-28-5

First Equinox Edition 2009

Printed in the United States

1 3 5 7 9 10 8 6 4 2

TABLE OF CONTENTS

PREFACE

In 1956, approximately a year after Professor Willmott's return from Indonesia, the Modern Indonesia Project published as an Interim Report his study of the national status of the Chinese in Indonesia. Subsequently, following helpful comments by Indonesian and Western scholars who had read this study and after having accumulated a considerable amount of additional data, Dr. Willmott undertook to refine and augment his earlier study, while also carrying it forward chronologically through 1958. The present monograph represents, then, a substantial expansion of his earlier Interim Report with considerable new data relating not only to the period 1955-1958 but also to the years 1900-1955.

Dr. Willmott is particularly well qualified to undertake this study. He was born in China, a British subject, in 1925, living there until 1946 when he came to the United States to enroll in Oberlin College, from which he received his B.A. in 1950. Prior to his stay in Indonesia, he spent a year of resident graduate study at the University of Michigan and three at Cornell University, the emphasis of his work being in sociology and social psychology. He arrived in Indonesia with a command of the Indonesian and Chinese languages and a substantial knowledge of Indonesian and Chinese culture. His sixteen months of field work in Indonesia (during 1954-1955) were followed by the investigation of relevant material lodged in the Cornell University Library.

Dr. Willmott received his Ph.D. degree in sociology from Cornell University in 1958, His major study, based upon his field research in Indonesia, *The Chinese of Semarang*, was published by Cornell University Press in 1960. Currently he is Research Associate at the Center for Community Studies at the University of Saskatchewan in Canada.

Dr. Willmott's studies are the first of several carried out by members of the Cornell Modern Indonesia Project relating to the Chinese minority in Indonesia. Others are due to be published during the course of the coming year.

Ithaca, New York   George McT. Kahin
September 15, 1961   Director

INTRODUCTION

During the period from May, 1954, to August, 1955, the writer was engaged in sociological research on Chinese community life in Central Java. He was interested in cultural change and assimilation in this minority group. It was apparent that an understanding of assimilation would require a prior knowledge of the national status and the national orientations of the Chinese, and materials were gathered with this in mind. In writing up this report, however, the author was aware that historians, economists, and other social scientists may also be interested in aspects of this problem. He has therefore endeavored to provide as broad a treatment of the subject as his abilities and sources permit.

With fellowships from the American and the Canadian Social Science Research Councils, the writer went to Indonesia to gather materials for a doctoral dissertation. The present report, however, was made possible by the financial support of the Cornell Modern Indonesia Project, during both the field research and the write-up periods.

Much of the present report is based on information and impressions gained from interviews and observations made by the writer during his stay in Indonesia. The majority of the material, however, comes from books, documents, and periodicals, mostly in the Indonesian language. Unfortunately, materials originating in China itself were not available to the author. English and Dutch as well as Indonesian sources were used in the preparation of chapters covering the historical background, but the contemporary materials were mostly Indonesian. As may be expected in a field so highly charged with emotion as that of minority problems, all reports and materials are subject to serious error arising out of the particular biases of the sources. Statistics are no exception in this respect. Although the writer has attempted to evaluate and cross-check materials wherever possible, most items of information were found in only one or two sources. Therefore, many errors have no doubt been included.

These various deficiencies and shortcomings should be kept in mind while reading this report. In cases where the writer had reason to doubt the complete reliability of a statement, he has used such warning expressions as "probably" and "it would seem that". But since it would be tedious to put every statement of fact in tentative form, the reader is invited to be his own skeptic and judge throughout.

The revised edition of this report attempts to cover developments only up to the summer of 1958 because materials were not available for the subsequent period. It should perhaps be mentioned here that two significant events have occurred in the interim. On May 14, 1959, the Government announced that no aliens would be permitted to engage in retail trade in small towns and villages after January 1, 1960. As a result, a large number of alien Chinese were forcibly moved to the larger towns and cities. Many returned to China. The Government of the People's Republic of China attempted to intervene, but to no avail. The second event, which occurred on January 20, 1960, was the exchange of ratifications of the Dual Citizenship Treaty. This means that the national status of all of the Chinese in Indonesia (and all of their descendants) will have been determined, through options, by January 20, 1962.

The romanization of Chinese names in this report follows the general usage in Indonesia. Most Indonesian Chinese persons and groups have adopted a Dutch romanization of their names as pronounced in one of the South Chinese dialects; for example, the Member of Parliament "Siauw Giok Tjhan", and the early Kuomintang organization "Soe Po Sia". On the other hand, a Wade-Giles romanization of the *Kuo Yü*, or mandarin pronunciation, is used by some; for example, the "Chung Hua Hui", which is an organization quite distinct from the "Tiong Hoa Hwe Koan", although the corresponding Chinese characters are identical.

Indonesian place names are spelled according to general usage in modern English-language publications; for example, "Surabaja", rather than "Soerabaja". The city of Djakarta is called by its former Dutch name, Batavia, wherever it is referred to in the period before its name was officially changed.

One other problem of terminology should be mentioned here. Many members of the Chinese minority group maintain that such terms as

"Indonesian", "native Indonesian", or "indigenous population" should not be used to exclude inhabitants who are of Chinese descent. They point out that the majority group itself is not descended from the original inhabitants of the archipelago, and that many Chinese families have been "Indonesians" for hundreds of years. Thus the use of such terms to apply to a group not including persons of Chinese descent may be considered to be discriminatory or offensive. While the present writer sympathizes with this point of view and disapproves of all invidious distinctions, he has found it impossible to find a suitable alternative terminology. He can only say that in using such terms in their exclusive sense, he does not intend to imply that Indonesian citizens of Chinese extraction are any less Indonesian than others.

In fact, the writer hopes that this report will be a contribution, not only to knowledge of the minority problem in Indonesia, but also to its solution.

Donald E. Willmott
January, 1961

THE POSITION OF THE CHINESE IN THE DUTCH EAST INDIES, 1900-1941

In 1908, the Tiong Hoa Hwe Koan, a leading Chinese organization of Batavia, was busying itself with a most unusual task. Its president had received a letter from a certain L.H.W. van Sandick, who had been a district officer in West Borneo and was now in Holland preparing a book on government policy towards the Chinese in the Netherlands East Indies. Van Sandick requested information and opinions from the Chinese notables of the Tiong Hoa Hwe Koan on fourteen points. Among them was the following: "Do Chinese who have become Dutch nationals by naturalization thereby lose their former citizenship? Or does the Chinese government continue to consider them as Chinese citizens?"

The officers of the Tiong Hoa Hwe Koan were no doubt impressed by the generally pro-Chinese outlook expressed in van Sandick's letter, and glad of an opportunity to publicize the aspirations of the Indies Chinese. To draft a reply, they appointed a special committee, including their own president, four eminent businessmen, and two grandees of the Dutch-appointed Chinese hierarchy. A month later the work of the committee was accepted at an extraordinary meeting of the Board of Directors and officers of the Tiong Hoa Hwe Koan. Questions about their organization and its affiliated schools, about legal restrictions on Chinese residents in the Indies, and about government policy towards the Chinese were answered at length. In each case a general "answer" was supplemented by "further information." On the question of citizenship, however, the reply was brief:

Answer: Concerning this situation we are unable to give a reply, because we do not know the existing law in China.

Further information: We cannot give any additional information.

All we can say is: Whether a Chinese who has been naturalized loses his former citizenship or not depends upon the opinion of the man himself. [1]

While this reply was perhaps somewhat less than completely candid, no one could have given a definite answer at that time.

And as we trace the history of the national status of the Indies Chinese, we shall see that six citizenship laws and four international treaties failed to settle the matter. Until the implementation of the Dual Citizenship Treaty with China has been completed, the status of Indonesian-born Chinese will remain about what it was fifty years, when the venerable leaders of the Tiong Hoa Hwe Koan said that it depended "upon the opinion of the man himself."

Traditional Dutch Policy as a Stimulus to Chinese Nationalism

The Chinese overseas, like their ancestors in China, had always been sharply divided by provincialism. In spite of their much greater residential proximity in overseas communities, barriers of dialect, custom, prejudice, and suspicion separated the Chinese into more or less exclusive groupings based on the district or even the village which was considered "home" in China proper. In the Indies there was a further division between the "Totoks", or recent immigrants, and the "Peranakans", who were local-born Chinese, most of whose parents were also local-born. The great majority of Peranakans had Indonesian grandmothers or great-grandmothers, and spoke Malay or a native Indies language in their homes.

Then, too, the overseas Chinese had never received any help from the Imperial Government of China, and were officially considered as outlaws until 1894, as emigration had been forbidden by law. No wonder, then, that the feeling of belonging to China as a nation had been almost non-existent among the Chinese throughout the several centuries of their life in the Indies.

The fact that the spirit of national solidarity spread quite rapidly among the Chinese in the Netherlands Indies after the turn of the century may be explained by the combined effects of two major factors: a common

---

1   Van Sandicks' letter and the answers given to it are found in the following source: Nio Joe Lan, Riwajat 40 Taon dari Tiong Hoa Hwe Koan-Batavia (1900-1939), Batavia, 1940, pp. 133-140 and 228 f.

dissatisfaction with the restrictions placed upon them by the Dutch Government, and a sudden influx of modernist and nationalist influences from China itself.

In comparison with the indigenous population, the Chinese enjoyed a generally privileged position in the colonial society of the Indies. Their grievances were none-the-less keenly felt. They were confined by law to the well-defined Chinese quarter in each town or city, and could not trade in the countryside or travel to another locality without requesting a pass from the authorities on each occasion. As the Chinese quarters became more and more crowded, they became increasingly intolerable. They were compared, with some justice, to the ghettos of Europe.

Although the Chinese were placed under the civil and commercial law applied to Europeans, they were subject to the criminal law and court system provided for the indigenous population. Among other disadvantages which this involved, they especially resented the *politie rol*, a police court in which it was difficult to secure justice because of the wide and arbitrary powers of the judges. Their resentment was magnified when, in 1899, the Japanese were given full legal equality with Europeans.

Another grievance was the lack of government provision for the education of Chinese children. Both the 1854 regulations setting up a limited school system for the indigenous population, and the wider educational provisions introduced with the new "ethical policy" at the turn of the century were interpreted to exclude the Chinese. They were admitted to European or "native" schools only in rare cases, and were even then charged higher school fees. Chinese schools received no subsidies. Yet the Chinese were paying as high taxes, or, in their opinion, even higher taxes than Europeans, for whom a separate school system was provided.[2]

There was an even more important economic stimulus to national solidarity, however. In 1900 the government ended its policy of farming out the opium trade to Chinese merchants, and instituted instead a government monopoly of opium sales and restrictions on its use. In

---

2 Fuller accounts of these and other grievances of the Indies Chinese may be found in the following sources:

P.H. Fromberg, "De Chineesche Beweging op Java", *Verspreide Geschriften*, Leiden, 1926, pp. 405-446.

Victor Purcell, *The Chinese in Southeast Asia*, London, 1951, pp. 507 f., 522-24, 528.

W. de Veer, *Chineezen Onder Hollandsche Vlag*, Amsterdam, 1908, pp. 1-66.

the same year it was decided to extend the government monopoly of pawnshops throughout the Indies, and to establish agricultural credit banks to provide loans to farmers at more reasonable rates than those which the private money-lenders, chiefly Chinese, had claimed. This meant the loss of an important source of revenue for the wealthy merchants, and the threat of serious competition in the money-lending sphere for a large section of the Chinese population, including even the small shopkeepers. These measures stimulated unity in the Chinese community vis-a-vis the government and, as we shall see, encouraged them to turn to the Chinese Imperial Government for support and protection.

Influences from China and the Rise of Nationalism among the Indies Chinese

With the factor of common dissatisfaction latent in the Chinese community, nationalism found fertile soil when its first seeds were brought from China just before the turn of the century. The humiliation of defeats and encroachments, first by the European powers, and then by Japan in the Sino-Japanese War of 1895, had inspired modernist and reformist movements among the intelligentsia in China, and contributed to anti-foreign mass movements among the peasantry. In 1898 the young Emperor Kuang Hsu, guided by the reformists, decreed a series of sweeping changes intended to strengthen and modernize the military, administrative, and educational systems. These were cut short by a *coup d'état* by the Empress Dowager, but after the Boxer Rebellion of 1900, even she was forced to carry out many similar reforms. Meanwhile, Sun Yat-sen was preaching nationalism and organizing revolution both in China and among the overseas Chinese.

These developments were bound to affect the Chinese in the Netherlands East Indies, because many of them were in constant communication with their relatives in China and other Asian countries, and because there was a good deal of travelling back and forth.

By the turn of the century, newspapers, periodicals, and books were already being published by Chinese in the Indies, mostly in the Malay language. This activity increased rapidly in the first two decades of the Twentieth Century. A large proportion of the Chinese press was dedicated to reviving interest in Chinese customs, Chinese history and culture, and a Chinese point of view among Peranakans. As China itself developed towards a modern national state, the Chinese press in the Indies added more and more political nationalism to its cultural nationalism.

Paralleling the development of the nationalist press was the rapid growth of Chinese nationalist education in the Indies. This began with the founding of the Tiong Hoa Hwe Koan in Batavia in 1900. This organization set out to promote Chinese nationalism on the basis of Confucianism, and to break down the barriers which separated Peranakans from Totoks and the various speech groups one from another. Within a few years at least a dozen Tiong Hoa Hwe Koan organizations were established in different parts of Java. By 1911 there were 93 of them scattered throughout the archipelago. Their main function was to operate Chinese schools. From the first these schools used Mandarin, or the national dialect, as the language of instruction, and employed teachers directly from China. They also served as wedding and funeral societies, and generally endeavored to promote adherence to Chinese customs, culture, and religion. Like the press, however, their orientation gradually shifted from cultural to political nationalism, and by 1925 they were ready to eliminate the promotion of Confucianism from their statement of purpose.[3]

The Chinese nationalist movement in the Indies was greatly stimulated by a series of visitors and emissaries from China. The first of these was K'ang Yu-wei, the leading reformist who escaped the Empress Dowager's purge in 1898 and thenceforth travelled among the overseas Chinese communities preaching nationalism and reform. His visit to Java in 1903 gave great impetus to Chinese community solidarity and a nationalist outlook in trade, education, and culture. In particular, he encouraged the establishment of schools, and set in motion a movement to eliminate the wearing of Javanese dress, the chewing of *sirih*, and other local customs among Peranakan women.

No doubt it was the success of exiled reformists and revolutionaries among overseas Chinese which awoke the Manchu Government to the potentialities of these communities as rich sources of political and economic support. In about 1905 the Manchu Government initiated an active campaign to win the loyalty and tap the wealth of the Chinese in Southeast Asia.

---

3 Nio Joe Lan, *op. cit., passim.*

The first Manchu emissary to arrive in Java was Lauw Soe Kie, an official of the Education Ministry. In 1906 he presented himself to Dutch authorities in the uniform of a Naval Admiral, and then proceeded to make a survey of Chinese schools in Java. He called together a conference of delegates from various Tiong Hoa Hwe Koan branches, and gave impetus to plans for a federation which would standardize and supervise Chinese education in the Indies. When the federation was established in the following year, an official arrived from China to take up the post of Inspector of Schools, a post created by the federation but paid for by the Manchu Government[4] At the same time, the Tiong Hoa Hwe Koan schools were invited to send their graduates to the Chi Nan Hsueh T'ang, a government school in Nanking, for secondary schooling. Up to the time of the 1911 revolution, about 200 Chinese from the Indies studied there, with all expenses paid by the Imperial Government.[*5]

More dramatic, however, were the visits of two Chinese naval vessels to Batavia, Semarang, and Surabaja, in 1907, 1909, and 1911. While Peranakans and Totoks came from far and wide to glory in the sight of modern warships manned entirely by smartly uniformed Chinese, the emissaries from China were creating closer political and commercial ties with local Chinese leaders. Referring to their first visit, a Peranakan newspaperman and local historian wrote:

> From the day on which that mission arrived, the feelings of the Chinese inhabitants of the South Seas towards their fatherland became more ardent. The name of the Emperor Kuang Hsü became ever more illustrious: he was considered to be the first Emperor who genuinely loved his people, for no previous Emperor had paid any attention to the overseas Chinese.[6]

These and numerous other missions from China gave great encouragement to the movement of leading Chinese merchants to establish Chambers of Commerce in major cities throughout the Indies between 1902 and 1911. Although the Chinese name of these organizations, "Sianghwee", literally means "commercial association", they were by no means confined to

---

4   Nio Joe Lan, *op. cit.*, pp. 80-82.
5   *Ibid.*, pp. 101-107.
6   *Boekoe Peringetan 1907-1937 Tiong Hwa Siang Hwee Semarang*, Semarang, 1937, p. 6.

commercial affairs only. In addition to local social and welfare work and the championing of Chinese business and community interests before Dutch government authorities, they formed the major link between the Chinese communities in the Indies and the governments of China, both Manchu and Republican. The Sianghwee of Semarang may be taken as an example. In the ten-year period from 1907 to 1917, it collected substantial contributions from its members ten times for flood relief in China and six times for direct support of the Chinese national treasury. It helped to sell either Chinese government bonds or shares for private enterprises in China fifteen times in the same period. Furthermore, the Semarang Sianghwee delegated its director to attend the 1913 conference in Peking, which chose a number of overseas Chinese representatives to sit in the new parliament. And on several occasions it requested the Chinese Government to intercede with the Dutch Government on behalf of the Indies Chinese.[7]

In 1908, Sun Yat-sen's revolutionary movement was reflected in the Indies by the founding of "Soe Po Sia" organizations in various cities. Beginning as study clubs with evening courses on national and international affairs, these groups became the center of Kuomintang organization and influence among Indies Chinese after the 1911 Revolution. In addition, a number of radical and secret nationalist organizations became active, such as the Ten Men League, the "Kong Tong" labor federation, the Blood and Iron Union, and the National Salvation Brigade. These organizations were considered dangerous by the Netherlands Indies Government. In 1920 they were suppressed or outlawed, after a series of violent disorders among the Chinese. Some of the leaders were deported, and the Chinese press in general was more closely supervised.[8]

The growth of the nationalist spirit was also evidenced in the anti-Japanese feelings and activities of Indies Chinese communities. Disturbances and boycotts against Japan began in 1912 and became more and more severe with each new Japanese infringement on Chinese sovereignty: the Twenty-one Demands of 1915, the occupation of Manchuria in 1931, and the Sino-Japanese War beginning in 1937. The Netherlands Indies Government, not wanting to offend Japan, took

---

7 *Ibid.*, pp. 6-13.
8 Liem Thian Joe, *Riwajat Semarang*, Semarang, c. 1933, pp. 247-249.

vigorous action to prevent such activities, even to the extent of forbidding the flying of the Chinese flag at half mast on the anniversary of the Twenty-one Demands.

Thus we have seen the successive rise of three manifestations of the nationalist movement: educational and cultural nationalism in the Tiong Hoa Hwe Koan organizations, commercial nationalism in the Sianghwee organizations, and political nationalism in the Soe Po Sia and the organizations which followed it. All of these, with the support of the local Chinese press, continually urged and petitioned the Netherlands Indies Government to improve the position of the Chinese.[9]

New Dutch Policy and Chinese Reactions

The Netherlands Indies Government set up a Bureau of Chinese Affairs in 1900. Officers of this Bureau, as well as such public champions of the Chinese as van Sandick, de Veer, and especially Fromberg, had been quick to sense that the interests of the Dutch Government lay in winning the allegiance of the Chinese. Stimulated by the counsels of these men, by fears of the growing influence of the Manchu Government, and by pressures from the Chinese community itself, the Government embarked upon a long-range policy of attraction. The pass system, which so limited the Chinese in their movements, was relaxed slightly in 1904, further slackened in 1910, and completely abolished in 1916. After 1916, the crowded Chinese quarters of many cities were permitted to extend their boundaries, and in 1919 in Java and 1926 in the Outer Provinces all restriction on residence came to an end. In 1914 the hated *politie rol* courts were abolished. In 1917 a new measure allowed certain individual Chinese or Indonesian subjects to "assimilate" themselves to Dutch legal status and participate in its privileges, but with so many qualifications that it did not satisfy Chinese demands for legal equality.

Probably most important in the long run was the establishment of the "H.C.S.", or Dutch-Chinese Schools, beginning in 1908. Unlike most of the schools provided for the indigenous population, the language of instruction in these schools was Dutch, and the curriculum was the same as in the European elementary schools. By 1914 there were

---

9   A comprehensive analysis of the rise of nationalism among the Indies Chinese may be found in the following source: Lea E. Williams, *Overseas Chinese Nationalism: The Genesis of the Pan-Chinese Movement in Indonesia, 1900-1916*. Glencoe, Illinois: The Free Press, 1960.

27 Dutch-Chinese Schools, and their numbers continued to expand throughout the period of Dutch rule. Many of the graduates of these schools were able to continue their education in Dutch-language secondary schools, and an increasing number went to Holland for a university training.

A few Chinese had been appointed to Municipal Advisory Councils ever since their establishment during the first decade of the century, and after 1909 the Chinese community was allowed to select some of its own representatives. In 1917 the Government announced that it was ready to establish a national advisory council, the Volksraad, and that Chinese would be given at least three of the sixty-one seats. This proved to be a touchstone for Chinese orientations.

On the initiative of H.H. Kan, a member of the Batavia Municipal Council, a conference of Chinese was called together in Semarang in mid-November, 1917, to discuss the question of Chinese representation in the Volksraad. With almost 700 delegates from more than 36 Chinese organizations throughout Java, including numerous officials and other notables, this was one of the biggest and most significant meetings ever held by the Chinese in the Indies. The debate was long and heated. It was clear that government policies had convinced a certain number of the delegates that by accepting their status as Dutch citizens and working through the advisory councils, the Chinese community could gradually achieve a satisfactory position in the colonial society. Opposed to this were the more ardent converts to Chinese nationalism. They believed that it was hopeless to expect concessions from the Dutch except through the struggle of the Chinese community itself, with the protection and, when necessary, the intercession of the Chinese Government. They were opposed to participation in the Volksraad and preferred to consider themselves as foreigners.

The conference finally decided, by majority vote, that the Chinese community should *not* send representatives into the Volksraad. This was the position which almost the entire Chinese press had already taken. It was a measure of the success of the Chinese nationalist movement to date.[10]

---

10 *Boekoe Peringetan 1907-1937 Tiong Hwa Siang Hwee Semarang,* p. 17; and Liem Thian Joe, *op. cit.,* pp. 235 f.

Throughout the 1920s and 1930s, the nationalist movement continued to thrive. This was in part due to the failure of the Indies Government to remove certain grievances still strongly felt by the Chinese. Peranakans resented that fact that although they were officially considered as Dutch subjects, most departments of the Government continued to class them as "foreign orientals". Because of the disabilities of the legal system provided for the native population, the Chinese community continued to demand total group assimilation to European legal status. The bitterness of this grievance was intensified by the fact that the Government once promised such assimilation but later announced that it would be impossible. Furthermore, Siamese were granted full legal assimilation in 1938, while the Japanese had enjoyed it since 1899. The Chinese continued to be dissatisfied also with the amount of Government education provided for their children, and they were convinced that their taxes were being assessed at discriminatory rates.[11]

While the Chinese nationalist movement was thus nourished by grievances imposed by the Dutch, it was also nurtured by support and direction supplied from China. Local Kuomintang associations throughout the Indies, headed by the Chinese Consul General in Batavia, formed the leading element in the movement. In addition to maintaining pressure on the Indies Government to improve the position of the Chinese, these organizations constantly encouraged closer ties with China. In 1932 the Chinese Government established an Overseas Affairs Commission to serve as a link with the Chinese abroad. The official solicitation of relief funds and contributions to the national treasury continued unabated. There was even an attempt to organize among the Indies Chinese an election of representatives to the Chinese National Congress, but this was suppressed by the Dutch authorities. The majority of Chinese newspapers in the colony were in the Malay language, but even these were predominantly nationalistic. This was indication that the Chinese nationalist movement in the Indies included not only the great majority of politically conscious Totoks, but a large proportion of the articulate Peranakans as well.[12]

Nevertheless, in spite of opposition from the China-oriented group, individual Chinese continued to accept appointments to the municipal

---

11 George McT. Kahin, *The Political Position of the Chinese in Indonesia* (M.A. thesis, political science) Stanford University, 1946, pp. 87-90.
12 *Ibid.*, pp. 79-87.

and provincial councils, and to the Volksraad after its opening in 1918. And throughout the 1920s, support for this position grew steadily. The increasing number of Chinese who received a Dutch education were acquiring also a Western outlook which alienated them from the Chinese nationalist movement. Those who were able to study in Holland were zealous Chinese nationalists while there, but on their return they usually found that Dutch society and culture were more congenial to them than was that of the nationalistic Totoks and their Peranakan supporters. There was also a good deal of rivalry between the students of the Chinese-language and Dutch-language schools, and this carried over into attitudes of mutual hostility later on.

Reflecting these developments, the "Chung Hua Hui" came into existence in 1927. This was organized and led by Dutch-educated intellectuals - mostly well-to-do business and professional people. The Dutch language was used in their meetings and conferences. The organization advocated the acceptance of Dutch citizenship, and specifically excluded Chinese Totoks from membership. They proposed to work for the interests of the Chinese community through political participation in the municipal and provincial councils and the Volksraad, and rejected any dependence upon the Chinese Government. Nevertheless, they took an interest in developments in China and remained enthusiastic advocates of cultural nationalism. For instance, they demanded that Chinese history and geography be taught in the Dutch-Chinese Schools. In 1939, the Chung Hua Hui held two elected seats in the Volksraad.[13]

The trend away from Chinese nationalism apparent in the Chung Hua Hui went one step farther in the "Partai Tionghoa Indonesia" (Chinese Party of Indonesia), which was established in 1932. To this group, Indonesia was the country of greatest importance for the Indies Chinese. Peranakans should invest all of their hopes in Indonesia, they said, and forget about China. They should work side by side with the other groups in the population, Indonesians, Eurasians and all, on the basis of common ideals. Thus the Partai Tionghoa Indonesia was anti-Dutch, and sought connections with the Indonesian rather than the Chinese nationalist movement. It held one elected seat in the Volksraad from 1935 to 1939.[14]

---

13 Liem Thian Joe, *op. cit.*, pp. 277f; and Kahin, *op. cit.*, pp. 93-95.
14 Souw Hong Tjoen, "Kenang-Kenangan pada Djubilium Lima-Puluh Tahun dari Tiong Hoa Hwee Koan Djakarta", *Hari-Ulang Ke-50 Tiong Hoa Hwee Koan Djakarta*, Djakarta, c. 1950, p. 15; and

Thus the period of Dutch rule came to an end with three national outlooks represented in the Chinese community. The Partai Tionghoa Indonesia, probably the smallest in numbers, centered all of its interest and hope in Indonesia alone. The Chung Hua Hui group was participating politically in the colonial society, but looking to China in cultural matters. The Chinese nationalist movement, on the other hand, was entirely oriented towards China in educational, cultural, and political matters. Yet it is nevertheless probably true that the majority of Chinese living in the Indies took no active interest in politics and did not join any one of these three movements.

Relations between Chinese and Indonesians under Dutch Rule

Under Dutch rule the Chinese had come to dominate the internal trade and commerce of the entire archipelago. They gathered the products of the land and sold them to big Dutch trading companies. Most of the small-scale manufacturing enterprises of the country were owned and managed by them. Except for the smallest shops and market stands, retailing was also largely in their hands. And Chinese shopkeepers, traders, and usurers remained the main source of credit for the Indonesian people, in spite of their unconscionably high rates of interest. This meant that the average Chinese was far better off than the average Indonesian, and that there were a conspicuous number of very wealthy Chinese, in contrast to the very few wealthy Indonesians. Furthermore, the advantageous economic position of the Chinese was accompanied by superiority attitudes and social exclusiveness.

The policy of the government, also, had the effect of setting the two communities apart and sharpening the differences in their interests. When residential segregation was finally abolished, educational segregation took its place. The whole series of concessions to the Chinese after 1900 amounted to preferential treatment, since Indonesians participated in very few of the new privileges. And until the last decade before World War II, the two communities were ruled under separate administrative systems. While the Dutch idealistically claimed that this policy was a matter of regulating each community according to its own customs and habits, the system was in effect a very successful example of the colonial

Kahin, *op. cit.*, pp. 96f.

practice of "divide and rule."

When the Volksraad was established, the Chinese were over-represented in comparison to their numbers in the total population. And Chinese members of this body, chiefly of the Dutch-oriented Chung Hua Hui group, often voted against the moderate Indonesian nationalists represented there. Except for a relatively small number of leftist Peranakans, and the supporters of the Partai Tionghoa Indonesia, the Chinese showed little sympathy for the Indonesian nationalist movement, and were therefore generally considered to be pro-Dutch.

Thus, although relations between Chinese and Indonesians were generally quite smooth, there was a latent resentment against the Chinese which could flare into violence when stimulated by local Indonesian leaders. It was the small Indonesian middle class – educated and professional people, religious leaders, and a few businessmen – among whom the position and attitudes of the Chinese were most bitterly resented. The great Indonesian nationalist organization, Sarekat Islam, was originally founded as an association of Javanese merchants whose purpose was to resist the competition of Chinese traders. The boycott movement which they launched in 1912 was accompanied by violent attacks on the Chinese quite beyond the policy of the leadership. Most serious of these were the anti-Chinese riots in Surakarta and Surabaja. At about the same time violence broke out between members of the Sarekat Islam and Chinese in Tangerang, which was to be the scene of a large-scale massacre of Chinese during the revolutionary war. In 1918 an anti-Chinese incident involving looting, arson, and murder occurred in Kudus, where the rivalry between Indonesian and Chinese kretek cigarette merchants and manufacturers was extremely bitter.[15] A similar incident occurred in Pekalongan in 1931.[16]

It should be emphasized that relations between the two communities were generally smooth and undisturbed. Outside the towns and cities they were often quite cordial. And everywhere there were a certain number of Chinese who maintained visiting relationships with Indonesian friends. Nevertheless, the causes for conflict between the two groups were deep, and when they came to the surface, hostility, anger, and even violence

---

15 Liem Thian Joe, *op. cit.*, p. 239
16 Boekoe peringeten 1907-1937 Tiong Hwa Hwee Semarang, p.18

could result. It was not a propitious background for the day when Indonesians would win the right to rule themselves – and the Chinese.

NATIONAL STATUS OF THE CHINESE UNDER DUTCH RULE, 1850-1949

Early Nationality Laws

The East Indian Government Act of 1854 defined the status of Chinese born in the Indies in two ways. On the one hand, Article 109 put them on a level with the indigenous population in legal and administrative matters, in contrast to the privileged position of Europeans. On the other hand, an article limiting government service to Dutch citizens referred to the existing Dutch law for a definition of citizenship. According to the civil law of the time, all persons born in the Netherlands or its colonies of domiciled parents were considered Dutch citizens, including persons of Chinese descent. This meant that the Indies Chinese, and Indonesians as well, could claim all of the prerogatives of Dutch citizenship while abroad, even though they were specifically excluded from them while in the colony. In Holland they could sue in the courts as citizens, and in Siam they could avoid the special taxes levied against the Chinese.[17]

By the citizenship law of 1892, however, the Indies Chinese were designated as "foreigners". This did not affect their position in the colony, but it made their status abroad very uncertain.[18]

Preparations for Consular Negotiations and Conflicting Citizenship Acts

With the rise of nationalism among the Chinese both in the Indies and in their home country in the first decade of the Twentieth Century, official and unofficial proposals were made urging the Netherlands Government to permit the stationing of Chinese consuls in the colony. An agreement between

---

17 Purcell, *op. cit.*, p. 514.
18 *Ibid.*

Japan and Holland in 1908, which provided for the opening of Japanese consulates in the colony, gave additional impetus to Chinese demands for consular representation. Although negotiations between the Chinese and Dutch Governments began in the same year, a consular agreement between them was not signed until 1911. The delay was due to differences over the crucial question of the national status of the Peranakan Chinese.

The Dutch made it clear from the beginning that they would not give China consular rights unless China conceded Dutch jurisdiction over the Peranakan Chinese. The Manchu Government's first step, therefore, was to assess the relative importance to itself of consular representation as against its claim to the allegiance of the Peranakans. During the winter of 1908-1909, Wang Kang Ky, secretary to Chinese Legation in Holland, toured the Indies for this purpose, and even held a semi-official census of the Chinese community in Surabaja. In March, 1909, the Sianghwee organizations of Semarang, Solo, and Jogjakarta undertook a census of the Chinese in Central Java, at the request of the Chinese Legation at the Hague. The following month the Secretary of the Peking Department of Education, Wang Ta-chen, made a tour of Java, ostensibly to study commercial conditions, but actually, according to a Chinese source, "to survey the situation of the Chinese community".[19]

At the same time, the Manchu Government promulgated a law on citizenship, no doubt partly to raise its bargaining power vis-a-vis Holland. This law, which was issued on March 28, 1909, claimed as a Chinese citizen every legal *or* extra-legal child of a Chinese father or mother, regardless of birthplace. This was the first official enactment of the principle of *jus sanguinis*, which the Chinese had always taken for granted as the basis of citizenship.

Apparently the Chinese Legation at the Hague expected to complete the negotiations over the consular agreement in a short time, for in November of the same year, 1909, Lu Cheng Hsiang, head of the Legation, wrote to the Sianghwee of Semarang requesting them to forward to Peking a nomination for the post of Consul General. According to his letter, the Dutch had already agreed to the opening of a Chinese consulate in the Indies.[20]

---

19 See Nio Joe Lan, *op. cit.*, p. 127; Purcell, *op. cit.*, p. 513; and *Boekoe Peringetan*, pp. 7 and 11.
20 *Boekoe Peringetan*, p. 7.

The Dutch, on the other hand, had everything to gain by postponing the agreement as long as possible, for they were gradually carrying out a policy designed to gain the allegiance of as many Chinese as possible. The pass system, which had been relaxed slightly in 1904, was further relaxed in 1910. Chinese were appointed to municipal councils, and beginning about 1909, each community could select its own representatives. Moreover, the first Dutch-Chinese Schools were just beginning instruction. It was expected that this policy, which was continued in further concessions later on, would win at least the passive allegiance of the Peranakan community.

On the other hand, the commercial, educational, and political activities of the few Chinese emissaries so far admitted to the Indies had had far-reaching effects in spreading the spirit of Chinese nationalism. The Dutch therefore had good reason to fear the consequences of allowing jurisdiction over the entire Indies Chinese population to be transferred to the Chinese Government. Before making a consular agreement, then, the Netherlands Government had to establish clear legal claim to the Indies-born Chinese, in order to counteract the effect of the newly-promulgated Chinese citizenship law.

This was accomplished in the Netherlands Citizenship Act S.296, of February 10, 1910. Instead of distinguishing only "citizens" and "foreigners", as in the law of 1892, the "inhabitants" of the Indies were not divided into "citizens" and "subjects". And Article 1 of the new law declared that all persons born in the Indies of" parents domiciled there were Dutch subjects even if not Dutch citizens.[21] This was an enactment of the principle of *jus soli*, in contradiction to the Chinese principle of *jus sanguinis*. It meant that the Indies-born Chinese, who had been assigned Chinese citizenship by Imperial decree just a year before, now acquired the status of Dutch subjects as well.

The Consular Convention of 1911

Once the obstacle of dual nationality was thus firmly established on its double foundation, the two sides took more than a year to come to an agreement about consular jurisdiction. Nationalist-minded Chinese in

---

21 Amry Vandenbosch, The *Dutch East Indies*, 2nd ed., Berkeley 1941, pp. 356ff, as cited in Purcell, *op. cit.*, p. 506.

the Indies raised a cry against the "forced naturalization" position of the Dutch negotiators, and demanded the protection of Chinese consuls. At the last minute the Semarang Sianghwee joined the Batavia Sianghwee in urging the Manchu Government not to sign any agreement requiring Chinese to become subjects of another nation.[22] Nevertheless, as the price for consular representation in the Indies, the Chinese Government did relinquish its claim to jurisdiction over the Peranakans.

Thus a Consular Convention was finally signed, and entered in the Dutch statute books as S. 487, on May 8, 1911. The Convention itself merely delineated the rights and duties of Chinese consuls in the Indies. It was the attached notes which bore on the question of citizenship. There it was agreed that the expression "citizen of" should be interpreted in each case according to the law of the country of domicile. Thus, in accordance with the Dutch law of 1910, the Peranakan Chinese were to be considered Dutch subjects as-long as they resided in the Netherlands Indies or Holland.

For most practical purposes, this ended the problem of dual nationality. The Dutch, as well as a considerable section of the Indies Chinese, considered that Peranakans were no longer Chinese citizens at all. That the problem was not finally solved, however, is evident both from a close legal analysis of the agreement and from later developments.

An eminent Chinese lawyer, Mr. Ko Tjay Sing, has pointed out that the notes attached to the Convention of 1911 state that its only purpose is to define the rights and duties of Chinese consuls. It was not intended, therefore, to define citizenship or to solve the problem of dual nationality. According to Mr. Ko's analysis, the Manchu Government did not concede its claim to the citizenship of the Peranakans, but merely agreed that the jurisdiction of its consuls should *not* extend to those persons who were *also* Dutch subjects according to Dutch law.[23]

Ambiguities Concerning the Position of Peranakans

It is indeed doubtful whether Manchu-appointed consuls actually would have limited their activities to matters concerning the Totok Chinese only. But due to the revolution which occurred in China just after the

---

22 *Boekoe Peringetan*, p. 16
23 Ko Tjay Sing, "De betekenis van de nota's van 1911 met betrekking tot het onderdaanschap", *Mededelingen Bond van Chinese Juristen in Indonesië*, Vol. II, Nos. 1/2,1949, pp. 1-12.

signing of the Convention, it fell to the new Republican Government to appoint consuls to the Indies, and it is apparent that these consuls never considered their duties to be so limited. They continually showed a lively interest in Chinese commerce and schools in the Indies, without regard to technicalities of legal jurisdiction, and the Sianghwee organizations served as unofficial consulates in cities where no official consul was posted.[24]

Certainly the Republican Government under Chiang Kai-shek never conceded that the Peranakans had lost their Chinese citizenship, even while residing in the colony. This was made clear by the passing of a new Chinese citizenship act in 1929, which reaffirmed the principle of *jus sanguinis*, and provided that a Chinese wishing to become a national of another country could only lose his Chinese citizenship with the permission of the Ministry of the Interior. It was also clearly indicated by China's attitude towards the Hague Convention on Citizenship, promulgated by a conference of more than forty nations in 1930. The Chinese Government refused to agree to Article 4, which prohibits any state from extending its diplomatic protection to one of its subjects living in any other state of which that person is also a subject.[25]

On the other hand, the Hague Convention did little to strengthen the Dutch claim. While it did affirm that every state has the sovereign right to determine who among its inhabitants shall be recognized as citizens, the Convention was not binding except upon its signatories; and even one of the great powers, the United States, refused to sign it.

The position of the Nanking Government on the question of citizenship is also illuminated by the fact that its consuls in the Indies repeatedly attempted to register all Chinese living there, both Totok and Peranakan. Each time the Netherlands Indies Government protested against the registration on the grounds that it violated the Consular Convention of 1911, the Chinese Government would apologetically maintain that a mistake had been made, and that the registration had been intended only for Totoks.[26]

In fact the dual nationality impasse between Holland and China was never solved. In May, 1945, the Netherlands and China concluded a

---

24 *Boekoe Peringetan*, pp. 19f., and Nio Joe Lan, *op. cit.*, pp. 128 and 143.
25 Soenario, *Masalah-Masalah Disekitar Soal Warganegara dan Orang Asing*, Djakarta, c. 1953, p. 10..
26 Purcell, *op. cit.*, p. 545.

treaty abrogating Dutch extra-territorial rights in China and regulating consular rights and duties. In Article 1 of that treaty, we find the two contracting parties solemnly recognizing each other's citizenship law, but politely refraining from making any provision: for the crucial cases in which the two laws were incompatible.

What happened, then, when a Peranakan Chinese decided to visit his ancestral home? He was issued a passport by the Dutch authorities, who, although careful not to recognize any Chinese jurisdiction over him, did suggest that he should obtain clearance from Chinese authorities. Proceeding to the Chinese consulate, then, he was issued a certificate in Chinese and English, which read:

Certificate for Overseas Chinese of Dual Nationality Returning to China

To Whom it May Concern:

This is to certify that the Bearer, M.............., in accordance with Chinese law, is still a Chinese National. However, he/she possesses a Netherlands Indies passport No.............due to his/her birth in that country. He/she is hereby permitted to return to China.[27]

---

1 Ko Tjay Sing, *op. cit.*, p. 11.

CHAPTER THREE
NATIONAL STATUS OF THE CHINESE UNDER THE REPUBLIC, 1945-1954

The Japanese Occupation

Before dealing with the main topic of this chapter, it will be well to consider briefly the position of the Chinese during the Japanese occupation. Soon after their invasion of the Indies in early 1942, the Japanese interned hundreds of the leaders of the nationalist Movement or of anti-Japanese activities among the Indies Chinese, and closed down all Chinese organizations. They then set up a single Chinese association in every locality, the "Hua Chiao Tsung Hui," with a central headquarters in Djakarta. Leaders of this organization were appointed by and responsible to the local Japanese commanders and to the office of Chinese affairs in Djakarta, the "Kakkio Han" (or, in Chinese, the "Hua Ch'iao Pan"), which issued regulations governing the Chinese community. Through these organizations, the Japanese restricted the movement and activities of the Chinese, and taxed and extorted large contributions from them for the Imperial war treasury. They also encouraged the growth of Indonesian-owned business at the expense of the Chinese, and removed Peranakan teachers and pupils from government schools.[1]

Thus the Indies Chinese, whether Peranakan or Totok, were all considered merely as *Hua Ch'iao*, or "overseas Chinese", by the Japanese. They were dealt with as a unified group separate from native Indonesians or Europeans. Their common opposition to and resentment towards the Japanese, and their newly-constituted monolithic community organization created a high degree of unity among the Indies Chinese.

---

2   G. William Skinner, *Report on the Chinese in Southeast Asia*, Cornell University, 1950, p. 65; and Purcell, *op. cit.*, pp. 551-553.

After the Japanese surrender, the Hua Ch'iao Tsung Hui organizations were reorganized under the name "Chung Hua Tsung Hui". In small towns they often remained the only important Chinese community organization, whereas in large towns and cities they took the form of a central federation of many separate organizations.

Chinese Reactions to the Revolutionary War

In brief anarchic periods during the Japanese invasion and later during the revolutionary war against the Dutch, the local people in many parts of Java made violent attacks on the Chinese. In some cases this took the form of looting, arising out of the economic needs of the masses and the jealousies of traders and small businessmen competing with the Chinese. In other cases Orthodox religious leaders led gangs or mobs to attempt the forcible conversion of the Chinese to Islam, Sometimes, too, murder and arson were resorted to in retaliation for real or supposed cooperation with the Dutch counter-revolutionary forces. And no doubt in all cases the attacks were at least partly fired by the prejudices and animosities which, as we have seen, had grown up between Indonesians and Chinese during the years of Dutch rule. Whatever the causes, the Chinese suffered severe losses of life and property, and the feelings of group solidarity of the Chinese community were further strengthened and extended.[2]

In the years 1946 to 1949 the situation in Indonesia was indeed a confusing one for the Chinese. There was intermittent heavy fighting between the Republican armies and the Dutch colonial forces. The Dutch imposed a strict economic blockade around the Republican areas, and business conditions were very unsettled. Republican forces found it necessary to destroy a large number of buildings, many of them Chinese, in a scorched-earth policy employed against the advancing Dutch forces.

A certain number of Chinese profited greatly from this situation. Some did so by supplying goods to the Dutch forces and cooperating closely with Dutch firms. Others contributed a good deal to the survival

---

1 Most of the material for this and the next two sections of Chapter III, covering the situation during the revolutionary war, was found in the following two sources:
   Clive E. Glover, *Reactions of the Indonesian Chinese to Two years of Dutch-Indonesian Conflict*, (research paper written for Prof. G. McT. Kahin's seminar), Johns Hopkins University, 1950, pp. 3-21. Purcell, op. cit., pp. 553-568.

of the Republic (as well as to their own affluence) by smuggling and blockade-running. Still others worked to the detriment of both sides by hoarding and black-marketeering. The illegal and extra-legal commerce of these people tended to arouse resentment towards the whole Chinese community, and their new shops, offices, warehouses, and residences gave the impression that all Chinese were benefitting from the uncertain conditions. Actually, those who gained were a relatively small minority. And since many of them had shown themselves equally opportunistic under the Japanese occupation, they are still looked down upon and somewhat isolated by the rest of the Chinese community. They form a sort of *nouveau riche* apart.

There was also a certain group, drawn mostly from the Dutch-trained intelligentsia and upper business circles, who were genuinely and actively pro-Dutch, either because of their respect for Western culture and adherence to Dutch ways, or because of their economic ties to the Dutch colonial economy.

For the majority of Chinese – shop-keepers, petty traders, and others – the chaotic conditions and economic hardships of the common people during the revolutionary years meant a slump in business activity and a decline in income. They did not especially like the Dutch, took almost no interest in the political issues involved in the struggle, and little understood the historical movement that was occurring around them. But what they wanted most of all was a return to the personal security and relative economic stability of pre-war times. They therefore tended to place their hopes in the return of Dutch rule. But in practice they tried to maintain as neutral a position as possible.

On the other hand, there was a small but not insignificant minority of Chinese of all classes who were sincere and active supporters of the Republican Government. Many sided with the independence movement because of sympathies arising out of closer contacts or friendships with the Indonesian people than were common among the Chinese. Others were ideologically anti-colonial, or idealistically revolutionary. A number of Certificates of Merit have been publicly presented to Peranakans who risked their lives and fortunes helping the guerrilla forces of the Republic. A certain number of Chinese served in the Republican armed forces. There were also a few Chinese holding positions at all levels of the Republican Government and in various political parties. At the time of the First

Dutch Military Action in 1947, for instance, two cabinet ministers were Peranakans, as was also a prominent leader of the Socialist Party, Tan Ling Djie.

Thus a wide range of attitudes towards the revolution was to be found among the Chinese. Their actions, however, did not always reflect their attitudes. Considerations of livelihood and personal safety were naturally more important to most of them than their particular orientation towards the politics of the revolution. Thus it is not surprising that in Dutch-held areas the Chinese acted in a generally pro-Dutch manner, while in Republican territory the opposite was the case. At the same time that the Chung Hua Tsung Hui (Central Chinese Association) of Dutch-held Batavia was making outspoken public attacks on the Republican regime for the treatment of Chinese in its territory, the Chung Hua Tsung Hui of Jogjakarta, the Republican capital, was collecting money and clothing for the Indonesian Army. Similarly, Chinese newspapers adjusted their policies to the different situations in which they found themselves.

Many well-to-do Chinese made (or paid) their way across the lines into Dutch territory. But while there was a large-scale exodus of Chinese from villages to towns or cities, this was usually a case of seeking the security of a sizeable Chinese community, rather than of choosing sides in the revolutionary struggle. Even the mass Chinese evacuation of Jogjakarta just before the return of the Republican Government in 1949 was not so much a sign of sympathy with the Dutch as a result of fears greatly magnified by the activities of irresponsible Indonesian groups who threatened the safety of the Chinese in terrorist pamphlets and posters.

In the summer of 1947 groups of armed Chinese, known as "Pao An Tui", were established for the protection of Chinese communities in many parts of Dutch-held territory. These were sanctioned by the Dutch, and in some cases armed by them. Their central headquarters was in Batavia, and by February 1949 they had branch units in at least three dozen cities and towns. Although some Republican leaders were willing to recognize the Pao An Tui, opposition to them came from the leftist trade unions, from the more anti-Chinese leaders, and from leading Chinese supporters of the Republic, such as Tjoa Sik Ien and Tan Ling Djie.[1] In any case, the Pao An Tui were suspected of being pro-Dutch, and the

---

2   *Sin Po*, Batavia, Dec. 15, 1947.

Republican Government at first took a firm stand against them. In doing so, it pointed out their similarity to the bitterly-resented European troops in China. However, at the beginning of 1948 it agreed in principle to the establishment of these Chinese self-defense units.

In the Chinese community itself there was a good deal of controversy over the Pao An Tui. A minority of leftist Chinese strongly opposed them, largely because of their close ties to the Kuomintang. And even among those who favored them, there were accusations that they were being misused for the benefit of special groups. In any case, there were no further outbreaks against the Chinese in Java, and the Pao An Tui were finally disbanded in the spring of 1949.

During the troubled times, however, many Chinese looked to China for protection. Local organizations made direct appeals to the Chinese Government for aid, and some Chinese newspapermen even proposed that China should send troops to Indonesia for this purpose.

Actions Taken by the Chinese Government

In view of the fact that China was engaged in a bitter civil war and was facing tremendous problems of reconstruction at home, the Nationalist Government paid a surprising amount of attention to the plight of the Indonesian Chinese.

The Chinese all over Indonesia were advised by Chinese authorities to maintain strict neutrality. The Chinese Consul General attempted to establish "safety zones" to be respected by both sides, where Chinese communities could assemble in times of danger. As neither side would agree to this, the Consul General then issued instructions to the Chinese in Republican territory to refuse to be evacuated outside the towns in areas of military operations. He advised them to gather in the buildings of Chinese schools or associations instead, and to fly the Chinese and Red Cross flags.

The Chinese Ministry of Foreign Affairs repeatedly made direct appeals to both the Dutch and the Indonesian Governments to safeguard the lives and property of the Chinese. The Nationalist Government appropriated a large sum of money for the relief of the Chinese victims of the war in Java. The Consul General visited different parts of the island to investigate and report on the situation of the Chinese in various localities. And the Chinese delegation to the United Nations continually implied that its support to the Republican cause was conditional on the proper treatment of Chinese by the Republican authorities. As might be expected, in its activities in relation to the Chinese in Indonesia at this time, the Chinese Government made no distinction between Totoks and Peranakans. The flow of commercial, educational and political emissaries from China continued as in pre-war times.

Actions Taken by the Indonesian Republic

Let us now look at the situation with regard to the Chinese from the point of view of the Indonesian authorities. Here was an important minority which, as we have seen, had always had a privileged position in the colonial society. They owned and managed almost the entire internal trade and commerce of the nation. Even though the majority of them had settled permanently in the Indies, and had Indonesian mothers or grandmothers, they had clung to their own ways and looked down on their fellow Asians. In the present situation they were an "uncertain quantity" . Many of them were helping the Dutch. Many felt allegiance only to China and were looking to the Nationalist Government for protection. And most of those who were neither Dutch cooperators nor Chinese patriots were indifferent as well to the Indonesian struggle for independence. Few indeed were active and loyal supporters of the Republic.

Under such circumstances it would not have been surprising if the Republican leaders had adopted a severe policy against the Chinese or had encouraged the attacks that were being made on them. But humanitarian ideals and practical considerations called for a different program. The Indonesian authorities decided, instead, to try to win the allegiance of as many of the Chinese as possible, and to make them an accepted part of Indonesian society.

When the Dutch undertook large-scale military action at the end of July, 1947, there occurred a new series of attacks by Indonesians against the Chinese. In the weeks that followed, Republican government authorities took various steps to defend and protect the Chinese. President Soekarno made a statement guaranteeing their safety, and this was backed by strict orders issued by Hatta, the Vice President, and Sjarifuddin, Prime Minister and concurrent Defense Minister. These orders prescribed the severest penalties, even execution, for persons guilty of maltreating Chinese or looting their property. Sjahrir, Sjarifuddin, and other high Republican leaders made public speeches regretting the anti-Chinese outbreaks and expressing sympathy for the victims of the scorched-earth policy. The Republican Information Service admitted the high casualties suffered by the Chinese, while pointing out that they had occurred only in the areas of military operations. The Government appropriated five million rupiahs for the relief of Chinese victims. And on the anniversary of the founding of the Chinese Republic, Chinese airplanes were permitted to fly over Republican territory in order to drop "goodwill" leaflets to the Chinese inhabitants.

The citizenship law promulgated by the Republican Government, which will be dealt with in the next section, was consistent with the policy of attracting and accepting the Chinese. Before concluding the present discussion, however, it should be pointed out that the policy was not always consistently carried out, especially by the lower ranks of Republican officers and officials.

In the first place, the Republican Government was in an extremely difficult financial position, as the economy had been disrupted by war and revolution and the Dutch had been enforcing a stringent blockade around the Republican areas. Under these conditions, it was necessary to obtain as much financial support as possible from the Chinese, in the form of contributions, taxes, and, in some areas, "special taxes." Many Chinese felt that an unfair and "discriminatory" amount was being required from them.

Secondly, the feelings against the Chinese arising out of the background of hostility and prejudice which we have outlined, often led officials and persons dealing with the Chinese to treat them arbitrarily or harshly. Legal and economic restrictions intended for aliens only (or in this case, Totoks), were sometimes applied to Peranakans. This, too, seriously jeopardized the official policy of attraction.

The Citizenship Act of 1946

Considering the uncertainties and divided loyalties of the Chinese, Indonesian authorities wisely decided to allow them freedom to choose whichever citizenship they preferred, since any legislation with predetermined categories would either force a certain number of China-minded Peranakans to become Indonesian citizens, or reject the aspirations of the Indonesian-minded group. Opinion was divided, however, as between two systems of opting for citizenship.

1) Under the "active system", Peranakan Chinese who wanted to be Indonesian citizens would have to make an official declaration rejecting Chinese citizenship. Those who did not, would remain foreigners, in the same category as the Totoks. Proponents of this system pointed out that only those with an earnest desire to identify themselves with Indonesia would take the trouble to go through the process required to gain citizenship in this manner. The indifferent would remain foreign. This would give some assurance of the loyalty of Chinese Indonesian citizens, and would promote their acceptance into Indonesian society.

   Some proponents of the active system saw it also as a way to solve another problem-the problem of bringing about a more equal distribution of economic benefits and opportunities between Chinese and Indonesians. This could only be done by restrictions on the economic activities of Chinese, and preferential treatment for an emergent Indonesian entrepreneurial class. Such a policy might be considered racial discrimination if applied against the Chinese as citizens. But if the citizenship law were such that most Chinese would remain Chinese subjects, legislation against foreign business in general might go a long way towards solving this problem.

2) Under the "passive system", all Chinese born in Indonesia and still residing there would be accepted as citizens, except those who took the trouble to make an official declaration rejecting Indonesian citizenship in favor of Chinese citizenship. This would mean that the large indifferent group, because of their passivity, would automatically become Indonesian citizens, leaving only the enthusiastically pro-Chinese Peranakans and Totoks as foreigners.

Proponents of this system pointed out that unless an unjustifiable mass expulsion of Chinese were resorted to, a large number of Chinese would remain a permanent part of the population. Such being the case, they considered it wise to extend citizenship to as many Chinese as possible. They were confident that through enlightened policies the state could win the allegiance of the majority of the Chinese community. On the other hand, they maintained that the active system would alienate even those Chinese already sympathetic to the Republic of Indonesia. Many also favored the passive system because it would minimize the number of Chinese over whom Chinese consuls could exercise jurisdiction, and through whom they might extend their influence in Indonesia.

The Citizenship Act which was finally passed on April 10, 1946, embodied the passive system. Under the terms of this act, which is summarized in Appendix I, Chinese who were born in Indonesia and who had resided there continuously for five years were automatically citizens of Indonesia. However, they were given the option of rejecting Indonesian citizenship in favor of Chinese citizenship. This could be done by presenting a formal declaration of repudiation to the Justice Department, through the local district court, before April 10, 1947. The expiration date for such options was later postponed for a year, and finally extended a second time to August 17, 1948. Other minor amendments were also made, but they did not affect the substance of the Act.

It must be remembered, however, that the territory under continuous Republican control during these years was limited to areas comprising about half of the island of Java and about two-thirds of Sumatra. The Chinese in these areas were faced with the necessity of deciding between the two citizenships – a necessity which was, however, largely mitigated by two factors. Firstly, the press reported a statement by the Nationalist Chinese Consul which assured the Chinese community that the acceptance of Indonesian citizenship would not imply the loss of Chinese nationality.[2] And secondly, before the final closing date for options, most Chinese were already convinced that the Republic would join the Dutch-sponsored Federated States in a wider Indonesian union which would have its own citizenship law. Considering these factors and the amount of anti-Chinese feeling at the time, it is probable that most of the Peranakans who considered themselves Chinese preferred not to reject Indonesian citizenship under this Act.

A curious feature of the 1946 Citizenship Act was that it established the principle of *jus soli* for determining the citizenship of the Chinese (and of others of foreign descent), but the principle of *jus sanguinis*

---

3   *Sin Po*, July 6, 1948.

for persons of Indonesian descent. Thus, in the hypothetical case of an Indonesian family living in China, the sons, grandsons, and great-grandsons born there would retain Indonesian citizenship (even if their wives and mothers were Chinese), provided only that they did not choose to become naturalized Chinese. It was just this feature in Chinese law which raised the problem of dual nationality, and which was thus an object of considerable criticism in Indonesia.

Developments in Dutch-held Territory

Between 1946 and 1949 the Dutch established a series of states in East and West Java, Madura, and the other islands of Indonesia, Each had its own elected and appointed parliament or council, but these were given little or no power to oppose Dutch policies. They were joined together in a federal system for which there was a Federal Consultative Assembly made up mostly of representatives of the participating states. Chinese were appointed to all of these government bodies, and many entered the civil service during this period.

In early 1948 the constitutional committee of the Federal Consultative Assembly discussed the question of citizenship. It was agreed that all persons of foreign descent who were born in Indonesia and had resided there for more than two years should be considered as Indonesian citizens, but a final decision on this matter was deferred until the opinions of the Chinese community could be ascertained. Since the proposal would not have allowed Peranakans the option of choosing Chinese citizenship, it doubtless received a good deal of opposition from certain quarters. In any case, the work of the committee was superceded and lost in the complicated constitutional developments which followed.

In the spring of 1948 it became apparent that the future government of Indonesia would have at least a fair measure of independence and that it would probably include the Republic as a component part. The Chinese press indicated a growing tendency on the part of Chinese to believe that their interests could only be protected by taking an active political part in the impending all-Indonesia government. Already the Dutch authorities had introduced a policy of strong support to Indonesian business enterprises, at the expense of the Chinese, and there was little reason to expect a more favorable attitude from the new government. The Chinese were ever more aware of the weakness of their position as a minority, and they feared that even as Indonesian citizens they might not be given equal rights with the rest of the population.

As a result, a new political association was formed in May, 1948-the "Persatuan Tionghoa", or Chinese Union. Even the newspaper Sin Po, which had so strongly opposed the participation of the Chung Hua Hui in the Volksraad of the thirties, was now in favor of political participation, and gave qualified support to the Persatuan Tionghoa.[3] The new organization outlined its main purposes as follows:[4]

1) To promote the progress of Indonesia and to co-operate with other nations.
2) To protect the interests of overseas Chinese without sacrificing the interests of the masses.
3) To strive for the principles of democracy.

The leaders of the Persatuan Tionghoa were convinced that only with the co-operation of the entire Chinese community, Peranakan and Totok, could Chinese interests be defended. Therefore, although the organization was made up mostly of Peranakans, it made an effort to win the support of the Totoks as well. It put forward the following proposal as one of its major policies:

Those Chinese who do not wish to accept Indonesian nationality should be free to select one of their own liking. China and Indonesia should sign a treaty as soon as possible, insuring the peoples of each country residing in the other country the treatment of the most favored nation's national.[5]

In general, however, the Persatuan Tionghoa proposed that Chinese should accept Indonesian nationality and fully participate in the rights and duties of citizenship. It insisted that the Chinese as a minority should have freedom to preserve their own language and culture, and specifically, that they should be allowed to maintain their own schools.

---

4 *Sin Po*, May 27, 1948.
5 *Sin Po*, May 24, 1948.
6 *Seng Hwo Pao*, Batavia, Nov. 11, 1948.

The Persatuan Tionghoa was accused of being pro-Dutch, largely because its founder, Thio Thiam Tjong, had been a personal friend and official advisor of van Mook, Lieutenant Governor of the Netherlands Indies during the first years of the revolutionary war. No doubt many other members were also Dutch sympathizers. It should be remembered, however, that the Chinese had already found that the policy of the post-war Dutch Government was to favor Indonesian businessmen. There was no longer reason to believe that Chinese would prosper more under a Dutch than an Indonesian government. In any case, it was now only political realism to accept and co-operate in the establishment of an independent Indonesian government. This was the stated aim of the Persatuan Tionghoa, as was also the complete abolition of colonialism. While accepting this frame-work, Chinese leaders, including those of the Persatuan Tionghoa, generally favored a federal type of state, in which Chinese would have greater political power in the smaller units, rather than a unitary state led by the Republicans of Jogjakarta.[6] As events turned out, however, the federal state established after the Round Table Conference at the end of 1949 was replaced by a unitary state before the end of 1950.

The Round Table Agreement on Citizenship

Four years of bitter struggle between Indonesia and the Netherlands came to an end in August 1949, when Indonesian and Dutch delegations met in a "round table conference" at the Hague. By the beginning of November they had worked out the terms under which Indonesia was to become a sovereign state. These included an agreement on citizenship which established the active system of obtaining Indonesian citizenship for persons of Dutch descent and the passive system for Chinese and others.[7]

The new Republic of the United States of Indonesia included the former Republic of Indonesia as well as the Dutch-established federal states. With the ratification of the Round Table Agreements by the Republican and various Federal legislatures, the new citizenship agreement became the law of the land. Under its terms, Chinese Peranakans all over Indonesia were

---

7   Glover, *op. cit.*, p. 37, citing information obtained by George McT. Kahin in an interview with one of the leaders of the Persatuan Tionghoa, August 6, 1948.

8   See Appendix II.

given a two-year period (until December 27, 1951) in which they could reject Indonesian citizenship if they wanted to be considered nationals of China. In effect this was the same system which had been applied to Chinese in Republican territory between 1946 and 1948. This group was now faced with the necessity of choosing between two citizenships for a second time.

As regards persons of Chinese descent, the only major difference between the Act of 1946 and the Round Table Agreements was in the status of persons born abroad but naturalized in the Indies as Dutch subjects. Under the former Act, such persons did not obtain Indonesian nationality, while under the new Agreement, they became Indonesian citizens if they were residing in Indonesia on December 27, 1949.

Ambiguities and Clarifications Concerning Citizenship

In August, 1950, the Provisional Constitution of the new unitary Republic of Indonesia was promulgated. In Article 5 it provided that matters of citizenship and naturalization were to be regulated by law. Article 144 stipulated that pending the promulgation of a new law, Indonesian citizenship would be determined by the provisions of the Round Table Agreement; and that anyone whose nationality was not defined by this agreement, but who had acquired citizenship under the previous law of the Republic, would remain an Indonesian citizen.[8]

Thus the Citizenship Act of 1946, together with its amendments, was to hold for a certain number of persons who had obtained Indonesian citizenship before December 27, 1949 – for instance, alien women who had married Indonesians, or foreigners who had become naturalized in that period. This was certainly only a very small group. But the legislation of the Republic (confined as it was to parts of Java and Sumatra) was not generally recognized as effective after the government for the whole of Indonesia was constituted at the end of 1949. Pending the passage of a new citizenship act, then, there was no strictly legal basis for deciding new cases which were not covered by the Round Table Agreements. Mr Sunario, a Member of Parliament who was to become the Minister of Foreign Affairs, wrote in 1953: "It is not known for certain whether or not

---

9 See Appendix III.

the Citizenship Act of 1946 is still in effect, and if it is, to what extent."[9] Another official, head of the Bureau of Minority Affairs, had stated in a radio address in 1951 that the Act on Citizenship was no longer in effect, but he referred to it as a clear indication of the "standpoint" of the Government on citizenship matters.[10]

Under such circumstances it is not surprising that there was a good deal of confusion regarding the legal position of the Chinese. In some parts of Java, for instance, local authorities thought that a Peranakan was not to be considered a citizen unless he could produce a certificate of citizenship. In the Bandung area, Chinese born in Indonesia of parents who had never obtained certificates of permanent residence during Dutch times were officially (but mistakenly) considered as Chinese subjects, along with their parents.

In a speech before a Chinese gathering in Surabaja in July, 1954, the Minister of Justice, Djody Gondokusomo, gave what was publicized in the press as a "clarification" or "new interpretation" of citizenship regulations. Actually, five of the categories of citizens which the Minister outlined were derived directly from the Round Table Agreement. Only the category including "alien women married to Indonesians after December 27, 1949, and children born to Indonesian parents after that date" was added to the Round Table provisions, apparently on the basis of the Citizenship Act of 1946. However, the Minister also stated that Chinese claiming Indonesian citizenship need only establish the fact of their birth in Indonesia, and should not be required to prove that their parents had resided continuously in Indonesia for ten years.[11] In September the Cabinet discussed and officially sanctioned the Justice Minister's statement. This undoubtedly helped to standardize the policies of central and local government departments and agencies. But since no citizenship law had yet been passed by parliament, the Chinese entitled to citizenship continued to face questions about their status.

In April 1955, a Dual Citizenship Treaty was signed by the foreign minister of Indonesia and China. This treaty will be discussed in detail

---

9   Soenario, *Masalah-Masalah Disekitar Soal Warganegara dan Orang Asing*, p. 9.

10 Soewahjo Soemodilogo, "Soal-soal disekitar Kewarganegaraan", *Siaran Kilat*, No. 22, issued by the Ministry of Information, Djakarta, c.1951, pp. 3 and 8. For a careful legal analysis demonstrating that the 1946 act was not generally in effect after 1949, see Mr. Dr. Ko Swan Sik, "Soal Kwearganegaraan dan Pembuktiannja", *Star Weekly*, No. 633, Feb. 15, 1958.

11 *Times of Indonesia*, Djakarta, July 19, 1954.

in the next chapter, but we may note here that it raised new uncertainties about the position of Chinese citizens of Indonesia. On May 17, 1955, the periodical *Utusan National* published a report that civil servants and officials connected with agrarian affairs had stopped all land transactions involving Chinese, pending further instructions as to the status of citizens of dual nationality. For some time there had been a loosening of regulations restricting the purchase and ownership of land by citizens of Chinese descent, but officials took the signing of the treaty as an indication that Chinese of dual nationality might be regarded as foreigners.[12]

Of even greater concern to many Peranakan citizens was the question as to whether they would still be allowed to vote in the coming elections. Various newspapers and public figures, especially those of the Opposition, had pointed out the possibility that Chinese of dual nationality might vote in Indonesia's national elections and then opt for Chinese citizenship under the provisions of the treaty. Opposition elements were concerned about such persons having the right to vote not only because it seemed unfair, but also because many of them might vote for the Indonesian Communist Party (PKI). In any case, Peranakan Chinese feared that they might be denied the right to vote on the grounds that their citizenship status would not be certain until the end of the option period in the treaty. They also feared that their status would be again in doubt after the twenty-year term of the treaty had expired.

An exchange of notes between the prime ministers of Indonesia and China in June 1955 helped to dispel the uncertainties which the signing of the treaty had raised. One paragraph of the notes provided that once a person had chosen his citizenship under the terms of the treaty, he would never be required to choose again. Another paragraph guaranteed that before the end of the two-year option period provided for in the treaty, the status of persons of dual nationality would not change until they had made their choice. This meant that Indonesian citizens of Chinese descent were to have the duties and privileges of citizenship, including the right to vote in the national elections.

In 1957, internal problems which brought Indonesia almost to the point of civil war resulted in a Presidential decree declaring a state of emergency. A new extra-parliamentary "cabinet of experts" was installed,

---

12 *Sin Min*, May 25, 1955.

but the military authorities gained increasingly wide powers. On June 4, a military decree concerning citizenship was issued "in the interests of public safety." The first of its three provisions will be discussed in a later section on proof of citizenship. The other two (as translated by this writer) were as follows:

> Section 2: A citizen of the Republic of Indonesia who possesses in his own name a passport or similar document issued by a foreign country and still in effect is considered no longer to be a citizen of the Republic of Indonesia.

> Section 3: A foreign woman who has married a citizen of the Republic of Indonesia since December 27, 1949, is to be treated as a citizen of Indonesia after having obtained confirmation from the Minister of Justice.

The wording of these provisions and the official explanation which accompanied them made it clear that the decree was intended only to standardize the policies of various government agencies until such time as a citizenship law was passed by the legislature. According to the provisional constitution, citizenship status could be regulated only by such a law. In order to quiet certain doubts and fears which were expressed in the press (especially the Chinese press), the Minister of Justice gave public assurances that the new regulation would change no one's legal status, and that it was promulgated with the knowledge of his Ministry.[13]

During 1957, it became more and more disadvantageous to be an alien Chinese in Indonesia. A large number of those who had rejected their Indonesian citizenship in the option period 1949-1951 began to regret it. Various Chinese newspapermen and politicians supported a suggestion that this group be allowed to reinstate themselves as Indonesian citizens in the option period provided for in the treaty with China. Government spokesmen made it clear, however, that those who had chosen Chinese citizenship would be given no opportunity to change their minds. Nevertheless, a certain number of Indonesia-born Chinese conveniently discovered that the rejection of their Indonesian citizenship

---

13 *Pedoman*, Djakarta, June 6, 1957.

(by themselves or by their parents) had not been strictly legal. The Justice Ministry announced that such persons might apply to the courts for reinstatement of their Indonesian citizenship.[14]

Many of those who applied for reinstatement were Chinese born in Indonesia after December 21, 1921. This was the group whose citizenship status was most often confused in the nine-year period before the passing of a citizenship law in 1958. Chinese parents, school authorities, government officials, and even Parliament itself demonstrated their ignorance about the status of this group.

For those born in Indonesia between 1921 and 1951, the law was clear enough. According to the Round Table Agreement, they were Indonesian citizens unless their parents had rejected that citizenship on their behalf. But many alien parents, through either ignorance or apathy, had neglected to reject their children's Indonesian citizenship. Others had been told by local authorities that since they were aliens, their children were aliens also, without the necessity of official rejections. Thus there was a considerable number of young citizens who were generally regarded as aliens. Their status as citizens was affirmed by the courts[15] and observed by the Immigration Department when it registered aliens. When military authorities ruled that only alien Chinese could attend Chinese schools, the Indonesia-born children of aliens who could not show rejection papers were required to attend national schools.[16] Yet earlier, in 1957, many aliens had been required to pay the alien head tax for all of their children, regardless of where or when they were born.[17] In the Alien Tax Bill, Parliament had included the unqualified provision that "children still under age have the citizenship status of their fathers."

While this provision clearly violated the Round Table Agreement as applied to many children born between 1921 and 1951, it was the first legislated ruling which applied to Chinese children born in Indonesia after 1951. This group had no legally defined status. According to the Citizenship Act of 1946, which was supposed to be the government "standpoint" even though not binding, all these persons would be Indonesian citizens. But in practice those whose parents were aliens were

---

14 *Hsin Pao*, Djakarta, August 7 and 9, 1957.
15 *Keng Po* (city edition), Djakarta, July 10, 1954.
16 *Sin Po*, Djakarta, January 21, 1958.
17 *Ibid.*

treated as aliens. The Alien Tax Bill thus gave support to current practice and, incidentally, presaged the Citizenship Act of 1958.

In addition to the events outlined above, other events could be cited to demonstrate the uncertainties surrounding the citizenship status of the Chinese in the years 1946-1958, These uncertainties, compounded with the chronic confusion about how to prove citizenship (which will be described in a later section), formed the basis for a considerable amount of discrimination against Indonesian citizens of Chinese descent. Spokesmen for the latter group, therefore, continually called for passage of a citizenship law and execution of the Dual Citizenship Treaty with China.

Draft Citizenship Act of 1954 and Its Opponents

In August, 1953, a coalition Cabinet was formed with Ali Sastroamidjojo as Prime Minister and the Nationalist Party (PNI) as the major participating party. This Cabinet promised to prepare a draft law on citizenship as quickly as possible, and it appointed a committee to advise the Government in this matter. Within a few months the committee had drafted a proposal, presumably based largely upon the Act of 1946, which incorporated the passive system of determining citizenship for Peranakans. Instead of presenting this draft bill to Parliament, however, the Government let it be known that it did not entirely agree with the draft and was studying important proposed changes.[18]

Early in 1954 the Government released a revised draft, and in March it was submitted to Parliament. Several features of the new plan, including substitution of a novel active system for the passive system of opting, met strong opposition. After a short time the Government withdrew the draft, explaining that its consideration by Parliament was to be postponed pending the outcome of negotiations with China on the question of dual citizenship.[19]

Nevertheless, on October 9, 1954, with the authorization of the President, the Minister of Justice officially sent the Government's draft bill back to Parliament, just three weeks before the opening of preliminary negotiations with China. Except for minor changes, the new draft bill

---

18 S.K., "Tentang Kewarganegaraan", *Sikap*, Djakarta, Vol. VII, No. 40, October 25, 1954, p. 8.
19 *Ibid.*

was identical to that withdrawn only a few months earlier. We shall here examine only the provisions concerning the status of persons of Chinese descent.

Aside from the naturalization provisions, Article 4 provided that only a foreigner who fulfilled all three of the following conditions might obtain Indonesian citizenship:[20]

1) He must have been born in Indonesia and must have his residence there.
2) His father must have been born in Indonesia, and must have resided there continuously for at least ten years either before or after his birth. (This provision applied to his mother, if, at the time of his birth, his parents were not legally married.)
3) Within one year after reaching eighteen years of age, he must go to the nearest Court of Justice and make an official declaration requesting Indonesian citizenship and repudiating his other citizenship.

These provisions were to apply only to persons born after December 27, 1949. In effect, they would mean that only third generation residents in Indonesia would be recognized as citizens, and then only if they made an official statement. This was an extension of the principle of *jus soli* unique in the history of citizenship legislation. No doubt anticipating considerable opposition on this point, the Government attached the following explanation to the draft;

For a country which allows foreigners to become residents in its territory, it is fitting that at a certain time the descendants of those foreigners should be received into the circle of its citizenry. To what extent and in what manner *jus soli* should be applied to persons who are not stateless depends upon the situation prevailing in each respective country.

Considering our aim of achieving a homogeneous People, this Draft does not force foreigners to become citizens. Persons of

---

20 See Appendix IV for full text of Article 4.

foreign descent who may be considered to regard Indonesia as their country, upon coming of age, are permitted to declare their desire to be Indonesian citizens and to reject their former nationality.

...*jus soli* extended only to the first generation gives not the slightest assurance that persons of foreign descent will regard Indonesia as their native land. If such persons have resided here for generations or if they have no country of origin, it may properly be accepted that they regard Indonesia as their own country.[21]

The reference to stateless persons is of practical significance here, because supporters of the Kuomintang who went to Indonesia as refugees were accepted as "stateless" by the Government authorities. Since the draft bill provided that persons born in Indonesia of parents having no nationality would automatically be Indonesian citizens, the children of Kuomintang Chinese might obtain citizenship with no problem of documentation or declaration at all, while Peranakans whose families had lived in Indonesia for many generations would experience considerable difficulty in obtaining citizenship. The irony of this situation was highlighted by the fact that Kuomintang Chinese were the least likely to feel a tie to Indonesia, because they were the newest arrivals and because Indonesia had recognized the People's Republic of China rather than the Nationalist Regime of Chiang Kai-shek. While this seeming injustice was pointed out by the opponents of the bill, it may be assumed that the Ministry of Justice, in framing the draft, had had no intention of favoring Kuomintang Chinese. Four prominent members of the latter group were deported by the Ministry of Justice about the same time that the draft bill was being discussed in Parliament.

A more serious objection to the two-generation *jus soli* provision was that, far from assuring loyalty, it would inconvenience and antagonize the very group who would be expected to take advantage of it. A prominent Chinese lawyer, Mr. Gouw Soei Tjiang, wrote:

Frankly, I do not agree with this (the Government's) position, because these things (loyalties) do not depend upon externals,

___

22 Unofficial translation.

such as second generation, active choice, and so on, but upon the atmosphere and situation which exists in a given country at a given time. If the atmosphere and situation in a given country are not suitable, an active system for second generation Residents, or any other system for residents of any number of generations, will not increase the homogeneity of the citizenry. But if the atmosphere and situation are suitable, then the first generation, or not necessarily even that, is enough to create homogeneous conditions among the citizenry.[22]

It was the following temporary, or transitional, provision of the draft bill, however, which aroused the most serious opposition:

Anyone who is already a citizen of Indonesia according to the provisions of Article 144 of the Provisional Constitution shall remain a citizen.
A citizen of Indonesia who has also another nationality, and who does not fulfil the qualifications of descent laid down in Article 4, will lose his Indonesian citizenship if within one year of the coming into effect of this act he does not make a declaration rejecting his other citizenship. This declaration must be made before the Court of Justice or the representative of the Republic of Indonesia at his place of residence. Declarations for those under eighteen years of age will be made by their parents or legal guardians.[23]

On the one hand, then, the new law would have confirmed the division of citizenship already carried out under the provisions of the Round Table Agreement. On the other hand, Chinese whose citizenship was thus already confirmed would have lost it again unless:

1) they could prove that their parents were born in the territory of Indonesia and had resided there for at least ten years continuously, or
2) they made an official declaration rejecting Chinese citizenship.

23 *Sin Min*, Semarang, Nov. 19, 1954, pp. 2-3
24 Unofficial translation.

Opponents of the bill were quick to point out the virtual impossibility of providing satisfactory evidence for the first of these conditions. Civil registration of the Chinese had not been initiated in Java until 1919, and in the Outer Islands not until 1926. Furthermore, registration records for many areas had been lost or destroyed during the revolutionary war. Thus very few Peranakans could produce birth certificates for their parents. In some areas, officials had already required that Chinese claiming the privileges of citizenship should produce proof that their parents had resided in Indonesia for ten years continuously, and such proof had been found to be extremely difficult to provide.

This being the case, most Peranakans would have had to appear at court to make their declaration if they were to avoid losing their Indonesian citizenship. But here the opponents of the bill pointed out the indifference of the majority of Peranakans to legal matters, their general ignorance of the issues involved, and their traditional aversion to contact with government authorities. They maintained that these factors would keep a very large number of Peranakans from taking any action. Thus a sizeable proportion of the Indonesian-born Chinese population - perhaps several hundred thousand, it was said- - would lose their Indonesian citizenship by default. Whether or not such a result was expected and desired by the framers of the bill, the opponents of the bill never failed to mention it. Chinese critics emphasized the loss to Indonesia of a potentially valuable sector of the population, while both Chinese and Indonesian opponents stressed the dangers of the much wider foreign jurisdiction and interference which it would involve. The proposed system was labeled "mass denationalization".

A closing article of the draft bill stated: "An Indonesian citizen residing in Indonesia is considered not to have any other citizenship."[24] This, of course, was directed towards the problem of dual nationality. It is evident from the explanations which were attached to the draft that the Government was quite aware that declarations renouncing Chinese citizenship would not actually nullify that citizenship under Chinese law. But for all practical purposes the clause just quoted would nullify China's claim to jurisdiction over Chinese residing in Indonesia who became citizens there just as the Dutch legislation of 1910 and the Consular Convention of 1911 had done.

---

25 Unofficial translation.

Nevertheless, critics of this clause pointed out that the problem of dual nationality could only be eliminated finally through an agreement with China, and that consideration of this bill on the very eve of negotiations with China was inopportune if not actually detrimental to the goodwill necessary for such negotiations.

As the new bill would not affect the status of other minorities (Dutch, Eurasian, Arab and Indian), but would raise new complications and obstacles for the Chinese community, many Peranakans considered it as a direct attack on their position. The influential Working Committee on Citizenship in Surabaja, claiming to represent all strata of the Chinese community in that city, made a public statement condemning the bill and calling for a return to the spirit of the Act of 1946.[25] A special committee of the widely-organized Peranakan political organization, BAPERKI (Badan Permusjawaratan Kewarganegaraan Indonesia)[26], issued a memorandum criticizing the draft in detail and opposing its "active system" clauses.[27] The most outspoken opponent of the bill was Siauw Giok Tjhan, Member of Parliament and leading figure in BAPERKI. Speaking of the new transitional clause in a press interview, he expressed the attitude of many Peranakans when he said:

> ...what had already ripened has been made raw again by these provisions. The fruits of nine years of efforts to cultivate the feelings of true citizenship among citizens of foreign descent,, especially citizens of Chinese descent, will be ruined, and the work will have to be started anew* The "minority complex" which we have tried to eliminate will be strengthened. The reason for this is that these provisions will raise again all the former confusion and unrest concerning the question of who, actually, is an Indonesian citizen.[28]

The Minister of Health, Dr. Lie Kiat Teng, also stated his opposition to the bill in a press interview, and maintained that so far as he knew it had never been discussed or approved by the Cabinet. Dr. Lie said that his

---

26 *Kuangpo*, Semarang, Dec. 18, 1954.
27 For a discussion of the character of BAPERKI, see below.
28 *Berita BAPERKI*, Djakarta, Vol. I, Nos. 7/8, October-November, 1954, pp. 2-3.
29 *Sin Min*, Semarang, Nov. 1, 1954

party, the Islamic Association Party of Indonesia (PSII), would continue to stand for the passive system as embodied in the Act of 1946.[29]

In the weeks that followed, party after party made it clear, through press releases and official spokesmen, that they opposed the bill. These included not only opposition parties - -the Masjumi (a major Islamic party), the Socialist Party (PSI), the Catholic Party, and the Protestant Party (Parkindo) - but the following Government-supporting parties as well* the Communist Party (PKI), the Islamic Association (PSII), and the Indonesian People's Union (SKI). The PKI and the SKI took the position that they could not vote in favor of the bill before the outcome of the negotiations with China was announced. On the other hand, no party made an official statement in support of the bill. It was generally supposed, however, that at least the Nationalist Party (PNI) and the party of the Minister of Justice would back it.

It was estimated that the parties opposing the bill could muster in Parliament at least 112 votes against it if it were put to a vote,[30] This would have been enough to make its defeat almost certain.

The bill was discussed only in sectional meetings of the Parliament, however, and not in full session. It was reported that one section passed a resolution to the effect that the majority of its members were in favor of the Government withdrawing the bill, while another section proposed that consideration of the bill should be postponed until after an agreement with China was reached.[31] In the face of such opposition, the Government decided to withdraw the bill. Not until three and one half years later did Parliament again debate a citizenship bill.

The 1958 Citizenship Act

In 1955 the Dual Citizenship Treaty with China was signed at the Bandung Conference, but the prospect of Indonesia's first national elections at the end of the year prevented Parliament and the Government from taking any further action on the question of citizenship. When the newly elected representatives gathered for the opening of Parliament in March 1956, a coalition cabinet had been formed, again with Ali Sastroamidjojo of the PNI at its head. In December, the Minister of Justice announced that

---

30 *Sin Min*, Nov. 11, 1954.
31 *Star Weekly*, Djakarta, Vol. IX, No. 465, Nov. 27, 1954.
32 *Sin Min*, Nov. 27, 1954.

he hoped to submit a new draft law on citizenship and naturalization to the cabinet in January 1957. About the same time, however, army revolts broke out in Sumatra. A cabinet crisis ensued. The cabinet resigned in March 1957, and President Soekarno proclaimed a state of war and siege. In April he installed an extra-parliamentary cabinet of "experts", with Djuanda as Prime Minister.

Both the Sastroamidjojo and the Djuanda cabinets sought parliamentary ratification of the Dual Citizenship Treaty with China, but strong forces in Parliament demanded that a citizenship law be passed first. It is likely that the Sastroamidjojo cabinet could not agree on a citizenship bill, since the coalition included parties with widely divergent views on the matter. The Djuanda cabinet approved a bill in November 1957, and in December forwarded it to Parliament in the middle of a debate on the Dual Citizenship Treaty. Parliament ratified the treaty soon after, but it did not take up the bill on citizenship and naturalization until six months later.

"Act No. 62 of the year 1958 Concerning Republic of Indonesia Citizenship" was passed on July 1, 1958, after four days of discussion in Parliament. Newspaper reports indicate that there was no serious opposition to the bill, and that it passed with only one dissenting vote. There were, however, eleven amendments, nine of which were passed by Parliament after having been accepted by the Government. Seven of the nine were proposed by the Communist Party, which had had no part in drafting the bill. None of the amendments constituted a major change in the purport of the law.

The text of the 1958 Citizenship Act may be found in Appendix V. Many of its sections involve minor technicalities or make provision for special cases such as illegitimate or adopted children. Here we shall discuss only those sections which have general significance for the status of the Chinese in Indonesia.

The Act opens by affirming the status quo: that is, it states that all people are Indonesian Citizens who have become citizens under laws, agreements, or regulations which have been promulgated since Indonesia's independence on August 17, 1945. Unlike the draft act of 1954, there is no requirement that persons of dual nationality make a court declaration if they want to keep their citizenship. Such a provision was made unnecessary, for the Chinese at least, by the ratification of the

Dual Citizenship Treaty with China, which does require active options. Thus the Act and the Treaty, taken together, embody one of the provisions which was strongly opposed in the 1954 debates, that is, the active option system for dual nationals who desire to maintain their Indonesian citizenship.

Section 4 of the 1958 Act contains a two-generation *jus soli* provision similar to that in the 1954 draft bill. An alien born and residing in Indonesia may apply for Indonesian citizenship if his father was also born in Indonesia and if he divests himself of his former citizenship. It may be noted that the official English translation of the act says that the alien may apply for Indonesian citizenship "if, upon the acquirement of the Republic of Indonesia citizenship, he has no other citizenship or if, at the time of application, he also submits a written statement abjuring any other citizenship he may possess under the legal provisions operative in his country of origin…" This translation is somewhat ambiguous in that the word "adjuring" may suggest that it is only the applicant's sworn rejection of his former citizenship which is required. What is actually meant is that the applicant must submit a statement which, under the legal provisions operative in his country of origin, divests him of his other citizenship. Since there is no way in which a person of Chinese descent can divest himself of his Chinese citizenship under Chinese law, except during the option period provided for in the Dual Citizenship Treaty, none of the Indonesian Chinese will be able to take advantage of this provision of the 1958 act.

The naturalization procedures outlined in Section 5 also are available only to those who can divest themselves of their former citizenship. Similarly, an alien woman cannot become an Indonesian citizen by marrying a citizen unless she loses her former citizenship. These various provisions of the 1958 citizenship act assure that no alien Chinese and none of their descendants can become Indonesian citizens after the close of the Treaty option period. This means that the only way in which the alien Chinese population of Indonesia can be reduced will be through measures amounting to mass deportation. Although representatives of BAPERKI and the Catholic Party argued in Parliament for naturalization procedures which would be open to alien Chinese, they were unable to suggest an alternative which would avoid the problem of dual citizenship.

The 1958 citizenship act makes it virtually impossible for dual citizenship to arise in the future. Aside from five, minor exceptions, it follows the principle of *jus sanguinis* - that is, the principle that one's citizenship derives from the citizenship of one's parents, and not from the geographical location of one's birthplace. Unlike Chinese law, however, this act declares that Indonesian citizenship is lost if any other citizenship is acquired either through marriage or in any other voluntary manner. In addition to preventing dual citizenship, the act includes many provisions designed to prevent Indonesian citizens from becoming stateless.

It may be of interest to note that the 1958 act incorporates, in only slightly modified form, all three provisions of the military decree on citizenship which was issued on June 4, 1957. Anyone who desires proof of his Indonesian citizenship is directed to apply to the District Court in the town where he resides. Alien women who marry Indonesians acquire Indonesian citizenship. And any Indonesian citizen who possesses in his own name a valid foreign passport or similar document loses his citizenship.

In summary, it may be said that the 1958 citizenship act confirmed the citizenship status which the Chinese had acquired through the 1946 Act and the Round Table Agreements. Furthermore, it projected this status quo into the future by making it impossible for Chinese aliens or their descendants to become citizens after the option period provided for in the Dual Citizenship Treaty with China.

Status of the Pro-Kuomintang Chinese
Neither the 1958 citizenship act nor the Dual Citizenship Treaty will do anything to clarify or settle the status of pro-Kuomintang Chinese aliens. As we have seen, members of this group are considered "stateless" by government agencies. They naturally prefer this to being considered citizens of the People's Republic of China - which is the only alternative in a country which does not recognize the government of Chiang Kai-shek, Pro-Kuomintang Chinese who were born in Indonesia did not reject Indonesian citizenship during the 1949-51 option period, because they feared that to do so might put them under the jurisdiction of Communist Chinese consuls. Similarly, the Dual Citizenship Treaty does not give them an opportunity to reject Indonesian citizenship in favor of Nationalist Chinese citizenship. Thus pro-Kuomintang Chinese who are dual citizens

will reject their Chinese citizenship in the new round of treaty options. On the other hand, the treaty does not apply to alien Kuomintang supporters, because they are not dual nationals. The Government has repeatedly made it clear that members of this group will continue to be considered stateless. At least until the end of 1958, "stateless" Chinese who wished to travel abroad were supplied with "stateless" passports by the Indonesian Government.

In parliamentary debates on the Dual Citizenship Treaty and the 1958 citizenship act, BAPERKI leader Siauw Giok Tjhan argued that under international law statelessness could not be adopted by a person at will, and that while the Government could offer political asylum, it could not unilaterally cancel citizenship of a nation whose government it recognized. Siauw repeatedly demanded, therefore, that pro-Kuomintang aliens be forced to obtain passports from the Communist Chinese consulates. Not even the PKI (Communist Party) supported this position, however, and it does not seem likely that it will be accepted by the Government in the future.

While the anti-foreign measures of the Government may force many "stateless" Chinese to seek refuge in Taiwan or other countries, their children born in Indonesia may become Indonesian citizens under the 1958 law or, if they are old enough, by options under the Dual Citizenship Treaty. Thus the problem of statelessness will not last beyond the present generation of immigrants.

THE DUAL CITIZENSHIP
TREATY WITH CHINA

L ittle information reached the press concerning the diplomatic contacts which led up to negotiations between Indonesia and China on the dual citizenship issue. The negotiations themselves were held in strict secrecy, and the authorities on both sides either denied or refused to confirm press reports and speculations concerning them. The main outlines of the developments leading up to the signing of the treaty, however, are fairly clear.

With the rapid rise of a powerful China under Communist leadership, the various governments of Southeast Asia became anxious concerning both the role that their sizeable Chinese minorities might play, and the influence and jurisdiction over them that the Peking Government might attempt to exercise.

The Indonesian government, therefore, proposed to the Government of the People's Republic of China that the two countries should negotiate a treaty to solve the problem of dual nationality. In early 1054 China agreed, but throughout the first half of that year the two governments could not agree on a date. The Indonesian Government was eager to hold the negotiations as soon as possible, no doubt partly because its own controversial citizenship bill was being delayed in the hope of an early settlement with China. On the other hand, China was in no hurry, and the Geneva Conference seemed to be absorbing the whole attention of its Foreign Ministry.

When Chou En-lai, Prime Minister and concurrently Foreign Minister of the People's Republic of China, visited India in July, 1954, Nehru discussed the question of dual nationality with him, probably at the request of the Indonesian Government. The London *Times* correspondent in New Delhi reported that Chou assured Nehru that China was ready to give up its claim to the citizenship of overseas Chinese of dual nationality, but this report was denied by Chinese authorities in Djakarta.[1] During Chou's visit to Burma, Prime Minister U Nu also raised the question of the dual nationality of Chinese there.

At the same time, a Draft Constitution was being discussed in China. It was adopted in September. Article 98 of this constitution reads: "The People's Republic of China protects the proper rights and interests of Chinese residents abroad." And Article 23 provides that the National People's Congress shall include deputies elected by "Chinese residents abroad."

On September 23, 1954, Chou En-lai gave a report on the work of the Government to the First National People's Congress. His report included these words:

> For our part, we are willing to urge overseas Chinese to respect the laws of the governments and the social customs of the countries in which they live. It is worth pointing out that the question of the nationality of overseas Chinese is one which the reactionary governments of China in the past never tried to solve. This placed overseas Chinese in a difficult situation and often led to discord between China and the countries concerned. To improve this situation, we are prepared to settle this question, and are ready to settle it first with the Southeast Asian countries which have established diplomatic relations with us.[2]

Southeast Asian governments were concerned over these indications of China's increased interest in the Chinese residing in their countries. At the same time, they were anxious to find out under what conditions China was willing to settle the question of dual nationality. When Ali Sastroamidjojo, Prime Minister of Indonesia, was visiting India in early October, it was reported that he helped Nehru prepare the topics and questions concerning which Nehru would seek information during his forthcoming trip to China. One such question would be: Was China

1 *Sin Min*, Semarang, Sept. 8, 1954.
2 *People's China*, Peking, No. 20, Oct. 16, 1954, p. 24.

willing to announce to Chinese living abroad, as India had done in the case of her subjects abroad, that they would no longer be able to have dual citizenship?[3] Thus it seems that Nehru may have played an important part in stimulating Chinese authorities to settle the dual nationality question in a manner satisfactory to the Southeast Asia nations.

As the time for direct negotiations between China and Indonesia drew close, two relevant pronouncements came from the Nationalist Chinese Government in Taiwan. On October 25, Chiang Kai-shek himself expressed his hope for the loyal support of the overseas Chinese of Southeast Asia. Speaking to a correspondent of the Singapore Straits Times, he said that the Chinese in the countries of Southeast Asia should take part in the efforts of the Kuomintang to regain mainland China.[4] The next day, after a challenge from India on the subject of citizenship, Kuomintang Ambassador to Canada, Liu Chieh, stated at a United Nations committee meeting that according to present Chinese (Nationalist) law, overseas Chinese are not considered Chinese nationals if they obtain the citizenship of another country.[5] Thus it was clear that the rival Chinese governments were competing not only tot the loyalty of overseas Chinese, but also for the goodwill of the governments of Southeast Asia and favorable public opinion the world over.

Preliminary negotiations on the Dual Citizenship Treaty finally opened on November 2. They were carried on in Peking until December 23, 1954 On the basis of the work done there, negotiations were continued in Djakarta and Bandung from March 29 to April 20, 1055, at the time of the Asian-African Conference. The Indonesian delegation was led by Sukardjo Wirjopranoto, head of the Asia and Pacific Bureau of the Ministry of Foreign Affairs. He was assisted by two lawyers, Suhardjo and S.H. Tajibnapis, and a secretariat consisting of Tamtomo, Tjhinhoikwet, A. Muhardjo, and Lie Chuan Sin. The Chinese delegation included Ambassador Huang Chen, Consul General Chao Chung Shih, and Lin Chao Nan.

During the negotiations, Indonesian officials repeatedly reported to the press that the talks were proceeding smoothly in an atmosphere of friendly co-operation, and that there were no disagreements in principle. No other details were given. At the beginning of December, however,

3   *Kuangpo*, Semarang, Oct. 2, 1954, and Oct. 7, 1954.
4   *Suara Merdeka*, Semarang, Oct. 28, 1954.
5   *Kuangpo*, Oct. 29, 1954.

the correspondent of the *Times of India* in Peking reported that it had already been decided that Chinese of dual nationality in Indonesia would be given a year in which to choose one citizenship or the other. Those preferring Indonesian citizenship would be required to make a statement repudiating their Chinese citizenship.[6]

While this did turn out to be the basic principle of the agreement as finally adopted, the Indonesian authorities were unwilling to confirm it at the time. It was essentially the same principle, involving the active system of opting, which was embodied in the Government's 1954 draft citizenship bill, and which had already aroused so much opposition. No doubt it was considered wise to postpone further excitement on this issue until after the Asian-African Conference in Bandung.

Through sources close to the negotiations, the present writer learned that the Chinese delegation was originally willing to recognize the *status quo* as to the citizenship of Chinese in Indonesia. That is, they would have been willing to draw up a treaty in which China would renounce its claim to all Peranakans who had become Indonesian citizens under the Act of 1946 or the Round Table Agreement. It was the Indonesian side which insisted on a new round of opting, this time according to the active system. This was consistent with the Government's desire to have as citizens only those Chinese who would be willing to make an official and public declaration repudiating their Chinese citizenship .

To the Chinese delegation, on the other hand, the merits of the passive system already carried out and those of the proposed active system may well have appeared to be of approximately equal value. The active system was likely to result in bringing more Chinese under the direct jurisdiction of the Government of the People's Republic of China. But it was sure to disappoint or even antagonize a good many Peranakans who were favorably disposed to the new regime in China.

Faced with advantages and disadvantages in either course, the Chinese side was no doubt willing to accept whichever system was proposed by the Indonesians. Even the generally anti-communist editors of *Keng Po* reported that the Chinese delegation had "given in" to almost every proposal of the Indonesian delegation.[7]

---

6   *Sin Min*, Dec. 4, 1954.
7   *Keng Po*, Djakarta, April 26, 1955.

Negotiations were hurried to an end during the first days of the Asian-African Conference. On April 22, 1955, before the close of the Conference, the treaty was signed by Sunario and Chou En-lai, Foreign Ministers of Indonesia and China.

Provisions of the Treaty on Dual Citizenship

The purpose of the treaty was to eliminate dual citizenship in cases where it existed and to prevent its occurrence in the future. Most of its provisions apply to persons who are at the same time citizens of Indonesia and of the People's Republic of China. This includes all persons of Chinese descent who acquired Indonesian nationality under the passive systems of the Act of 1946 and the Round Table Agreement. It does not include those who were born in China and were never naturalized as Dutch subjects, or those who rejected Indonesian citizenship during the opting periods of 1946-48 and 1949-51. These latter, being Chinese citizens only, were given no further choice in the matter.

Under the terms of this treaty,[8] adults having the dual nationality of the two countries would be given a period of two years in which to choose the citizenship of one or the other. They would be required either to repudiate Chinese citizenship in a declaration before designated Indonesian authorities, or to repudiate Indonesian citizenship before designated Chinese authorities. For the purpose of registering such declarations, either country could set up temporary offices in various parts of the other country after obtaining permission from the host government.

Persons of dual nationality who neglected to choose one citizenship or the other within the two year period would automatically acquire only the nationality of their forefathers. Those of dual nationality who were not yet of age would have to choose their citizenship within one year after their eighteenth birthday or their marriage. Before choosing, they would be considered to have only the nationality of their fathers.

In the future, all children born in Indonesia of alien Chinese parents would acquire Chinese citizenship, while those born in China of Indonesian parents would be Indonesian.[9]

---

8   See Appendix VI for the text.
9   *Keng Po*, May 2, 1955.

A novel feature of the treaty was the absolute equality it would provide between men and women. A choice of citizenship by a husband of dual nationality would not apply to his wife, who, if also of dual nationality, would have to make her own choice. In a marriage between an Indonesian and a Chinese, neither party would automatically acquire the citizenship of the other; they could remain different nationalities, or either one could acquire the citizenship of the other by applying to the proper authorities.

One of the final provisions was that each party should undertake to instruct its own subjects residing in the territory of the other to follow the local laws and customs, but not to take any part in local politics. Each party also agreed to protect, according to its own laws, the "legal rights and interests" of the citizens of the other country residing within its borders.

Reactions of Various Parties to the Treaty

The treaty was hailed as a great success by Government-supporting politicians, correspondents, and editors in Indonesia. The central council of the Nationalist Party (PNI) issued a statement declaring their full support. Pointing out that their party is in favor of creating a unified citizenry with no differences according to race, they stated that the present treaty would remove the basis for the continuing existence of minorities.

The Central Committee of the Communist Party (PKI) also issued a supporting statement. Although the treaty was neither complete nor perfect, they said, it would form the basis for a wise and democratic solution of the problem. Admittedly the passive system of options was easier and simpler than the active system provided for in the treaty, but the passive system had neither solved the problem of dual nationality nor the minority problems associated with it. Charging that the fact of dual nationality had been used by certain groups to incite discrimination and bring about racial oppression, the statement continued:

> The elimination of dual nationality will mean also the elimination, or the great reduction, of the factors which continually create tension between Chinese citizens of Indonesia and other citizens....
> It is certain that an active and unconfused attitude (as would be demonstrated in active options) will be of great help in eliminating the prejudices of that part of the Indonesian people who are

victims of the divide - and-rule tactics of the imperialists and their accomplices.[10]

While generally supporting the active option system, the Communist Party statement asked that the question of who held dual citizenship (and who would not be required to opt) should be settled by an exchange of notes prior to ratification of the treaty.

In addition to such general support, the treaty also met with a great deal of opposition as soon as its text was released. Even many Government supporters criticized various aspects of the treaty. For instance, Dr. Diapari, head of the Indonesian People's Union (SKI), found it far from satisfactory. He proposed consultations among the Government parties to discuss the problems involved. Specifically, he did not approve of changing from a passive to an active system, because of the likelihood that a large number of Chinese would thereby lose their Indonesian citizenship. Dr. Diapari expressed his concern over the possible results of having too many foreigners living in Indonesia.[11]

The opposition parties were, of course, much more outspoken in their criticism of the treaty. Jusuf Wibisono, speaking for the Masjumi, expressed three major objections: the objection in principle that the treaty was contrary to the Provisional Constitution, the Political Manifesto of 1945, the Citizenship Act of 1946, and the Round Table Agreement of 1949; the moral objection that the treaty would sacrifice to China many Chinese whom the Indonesian Government had hitherto considered as friends; and the practical objection that registration of over a million Chinese would involve tremendous difficulties, complicated further by the likelihood of a good deal of corruption in the process.[12]

The Secretariat of the Indonesian Socialist Party (PSI) issued a statement rejecting the treaty on grounds similar to those outlined by Dr. Diapari and Mr. Wibisono. It maintained that Indonesia should have demanded that China recognize the Indonesian citizenship of Chinese who had accepted it under the passive system, and release them from Chinese citizenship.[13]

---

10 *Harian Rakjat*, May 17, 1955.
11 *Keng Po*, April 30, 1955.
12 *Keng Po*, April 27, 1955.
13 *Keng Po*, April 30, 1955.

The Catholic Party (Partai Katolik) in an official rejection of the treaty, maintained that it was not only unconstitutional, but that it would violate the United Nations' Universal Declaration of Human Rights, which had been accepted by Indonesia, and which guarantees that no person's citizenship may be revoked by any law or treaty. The Catholic Party also opposed the provisions of the treaty which would permit members of one family to have different citizenships, especially husbands and wives. This was considered contrary to moral principles in general and to the principle of family unity in particular.[14]

Similarly, the Protestant Party (Parkindo), the anti-Stalinist communist party (Murba), the Hazairin faction of the Union for a Greater Indonesia (PIR), and other smaller parties went on record against the treaty.

Beyond the objections which they stated publicly, anti-communist politicians were opposing the treaty partly because it would involve the establishment throughout Indonesia of registration offices manned by personnel of the People's Republic of China. It was feared that these might also be used for purposes other than registration.

Reactions of Indonesian Chinese to the Treaty

The feelings of the Indonesian Chinese community towards the treaty were much more complicated than they had been towards the draft citizenship bill just a few months before. While articulate Peranakans had been almost unanimous in opposing the draft, they were not so sure about the treaty. Most of them still disliked the prospect of having to go through another option period, and objected to an active system on the grounds that it would cause a substantial section of their community to lose their Indonesian citizenship. On the other hand, many of the objectionable features of the draft bill were not to be found in the treaty, especially the two-generation *jus soli* provision. Then too, the treaty seemed to promise a final resolution of the thorny problem of dual nationality, whereas no unilateral bill could do so. Finally, one party to the treaty was the People's Republic of China. As will be explained in a later chapter, many of those who most eagerly demand only Indonesian citizenship are also sympathetic towards Mao Tze-tung's new regime in China and proud of its accomplishments. They are eager to promote good relations between

14 *Keng Po*, May 14, 1955.

the two countries. It would have been uncomfortable indeed for them to oppose a treaty signed by the Government of the People's Republic of China and by the Indonesian Government which had been most friendly towards that country to date.

Thus many Chinese viewed the treaty with mixed feelings. Those who supported it admitted its weaknesses. Those who opposed it did so cautiously, and with many good words about the intentions of the contracting parties. Many preferred to take no stand at all. A popular solution was to support the treaty, while advocating radical changes in its practical execution.

Let us take, for example, the pro-Peking Semarang newspaper, *Sin Min*. Thus paper had published many news articles and reports of speeches attacking the draft citizenship act of 1954, and although its policy was generally to support the Government it had criticized the bill editorially. On the treaty issue, however, it took no editorial stand, but published reports of speeches by both the supporters and the more cautious opponents of the treaty. Its nearest approach to taking a position was in a column written by one of its Djakarta correspondents, headed: "Find a simple way to carry out the Chou-Sunario Treaty."

In this column the writer raised no objection to the treaty. But he drew attention to the importance of what he called the "psychological factor," in the following words:

...the feelings of those who have already clearly chosen Indonesian citizenship and who have shown their readiness to serve the Country and the People of Indonesia, *must not be offended or injured.*

...And in the execution of the Chou-Sunario treaty, in our opinion, a simple way can still be found to eradicate the impression that the Government is intentionally making the position of Indonesian citizens of Chinese descent more difficult.[15]

The "simple way" proposed by this columnist was to recognize as Indonesian citizens *without* dual nationality all those persons of Chinese

15 *Sin Min*, Semarang, May 12, 1955.

descent who have served as Cabinet Ministers, Members of Parliament, and government employees, as well as those who have been registered as voters and gone to the polls. This would release a very large proportion of the Peranakan population from the necessity of making another option, and would thus eliminate one of the major objections to the treaty. So far as the present writer is aware, this was the first time that this proposal appeared in the press. The proposal is said to have been originated by Siauw Giok Tjhan, however. It was to be taken up seriously by the Government later on.

The anti-communist *Kuangpo*, another Semarang newspaper, which generally supports the Government, took a clear but discreet stand against the treaty. In addition to objecting to the expected denationalization of many passive citizens of Chinese descent, an editorial in this paper also emphasized the psychological factor, as follows:

> We who regard the problem of choosing Indonesian citizenship not from considerations of profit and loss, but entirely on the basis of a realization that by force of nature we are sons of Indonesia who for several generations have had no legal connection with China whatsoever - we feel rather disappointed that in order to defend our new citizenship we shall have to go through another formality. We are not disappointed because of the formality *as such*, but because we feel that the formality is not necessary for us, and that we have no ties with the outside world which need to be cut off by going through another formality.[16]

The two most important Peranakan newspapers in Djakarta took opposite sides on this issue, as on most others. The *Sin Po*, a pro-Peking paper, generally favored the treaty. The *Keng Po*, which favored neither the Communists nor the Kuomintang in China politics but generally sided with the opposition parties in Indonesia at that time (Masjumi, PSI, etc.) vigorously opposed the treaty. The *Keng Po* suggested editorially that revoking the Indonesian citizenship of Peranakans who failed to repudiate Chinese citizenship would create a serious problem

---

16 *Kuangpo*, Semarang, April 27, 1955.

of "displaced persons."[17]. Two weeks later, Mr. Yap Thiam Hin, a leading figure in Chinese Protestant circles and an officer of BAPERKI, gave an even more alarming picture of the possible consequences of the treaty. The *Keng Po* reported:

> Mr. Yap…stated his opinion that the methods proposed in the treaty would have grave social consequences, which could even endanger the stability and security of Indonesia itself. He believed that 80% of the people of Chinese descent, who had already become Indonesian citizens, would now be "uprooted" like displaced persons, because without knowing it they would become foreigners or stateless persons if the treaty were ratified. Their livelihood, judging from the fact that even as citizens it had been interfered with and made difficult, would become even harder, and this might raise criminality, etc. Where would they be sent – those hundred of thousands of farmers in Tangerang, Bekasi, Bangka, Kalimantan, etc. who, as foreigners or stateless persons would no longer be able to cultivate the soil because of the difficulty of getting land or because their right to rent land would have been snatched away?[18]

The majority of members of BAPERKI, however, took a more moderate and realistic view of the treaty, no doubt partly because of a general orientation more sympathetic both to the new regime in China and to the government parties in Indonesia. BAPERKI issued a statement[19] in which it cautiously advanced a number of critical "impressions" of the treaty: that it seemed intended to reduce the number of Indonesian citizens of Chinese descent; that the fact that it could be abrogated by either party after twenty years might give citizens of Chinese descent a doubtful status which could serve as a continuing basis for discrimination; that the treaty might nullify the efforts of the Indonesian Government to make good citizens of its subjects of foreign descent; and that it might undermine public and international faith in the legal foundations of the Government, since it was contrary to the constitution and the law to date. Instead of opposing the treaty, however, the BAPERKI statement called upon the

---

17 *Keng Po*, Djakarta, April 26, 1955.
18 *Keng Po*, May 9, 1955.
19 *Keng Po*, April 29, 1955.

Government to interpret and carry it out in such a way as to guarantee the continued Indonesian citizenship of all persons who had already acquired it.

The influential Working Committee on Citizenship in Surabaja issued a stronger statement outlining similar objections to the treaty. It included a warning about the dangers of "international interference" if the number of Chinese subjects in Indonesia should become too great. (This was indicative of a more critical attitude towards the Peking regime than that of BAPERKI.) Finally, it reported that by a majority vote the Committee had decided to oppose the treaty, at least so long as its objectionable features were not removed by any subsequent exchange of notes or official clarifications.[20]

Typical of those most favorably disposed towards the treaty was Dr. Tjoa Sik len, who had represented Indonesia at the United Nations at a time when the Republic, hard-pressed by Dutch forces, was struggling for world recognition and support. He was one of the influential Peranakan leaders most sympathetic toward the new regime in China. Dr. Tjoa had been opposed to the active system, but personal discussions with Indonesian and Chinese authorities after the treaty was signed convinced him of its desirability as a method of minimizing prejudice and discrimination against Peranakan citizens. In a public speech and a statement to the press, Dr Tjoa analyzed the treaty in detail, pointing out its strengths and weaknesses. He maintained, however, that talk of displaced persons and statelessness was premature, and insisted upon reserving final judgment until official clarifications had been given, particularly concerning the question of who should be considered to have dual nationality.[21]

The most outstanding of the cautious opponents of the treaty was Siauw Giok Tjhan, Member of Parliament, and head of BAPERKI. Although Siauw ardently identifies himself with Indonesia, he is an admirer of Mao Tze-tung's regime and an avowed enemy of the Kuomintang Chinese in Indonesia. In an interview with the press, he listed eleven shortcomings of the treaty, including many which have been mentioned above. He expressed his hope that the Indonesian Government would establish the principle that all of its citizens of Chinese descent should retain their

---

20 *Kuangpo*, Semarang, May 21, 1955.
21 *Sin Min*, Semarang, April 29, 1955, and May 17, 1955.

Indonesian citizenship.[22]

While differing on the merits of the treaty itself, Peranakans were unanimous in their fear that the signing of the treaty might raise uncertainties about their rights as citizens, at least until the end of the two-year option period They were united, therefore, in their desire for the Government to issue a directive guaranteeing the continuation of their full rights as citizens, in spite of the uncertainties raised by the treaty. Siauw Giok Tjhan, in parliamentary questions to the Cabinet, urged the Government to do so.[23]

Exchange of Notes Concerning the Treaty
On June 3, 1955, during Prime Minister Ali Sastroamidjojo's visit to Peking, an exchange of notes concerning the Dual Citizenship Treaty took place. Signed by the Prime Ministers of the two countries, this document represents a supplement which was to be ratified and to come into effect along with the treaty itself.

The content of the notes made it immediately apparent that the two Governments were well aware of the opposition the treaty had aroused in various groups, and that they now intended to modify it in such a way as to remove certain objections. It had become doubtful whether the treaty could be accepted by the Indonesian Parliament, and in any case both governments wanted to have the good will of the Peranakan Chinese.

The first paragraph of the document restates the purposes of the treaty, while another provides for a Joint Committee to be set up in Djakarta for the purpose of discussing and planning its execution. The other three paragraphs represent interpretations and elaborations of the treaty. Two of these were designed to remove ambiguities about the status of Indonesian citizens of Chinese descent before the option period and after the twenty-year term of the treaty, as was explained in the previous chapter.

The most remarkable provision of the notes, however, was Paragraph 2, which reads as follows:

The Government of the People's Republic of China and the

---

22 *Keng Po*, April 28, 1955.
23 *Sin Min*, May 25, 1955:

Government of the Republic of Indonesia agree that among those who are at the same time citizens of Indonesia and of the People's Republic of China there is a certain group who may be considered to have only one citizenship and not to have dual citizenship, because, in the opinion of the Government of the Republic of Indonesia, their social and political position demonstrates that they have spontaneously (in an implicit manner) renounced the citizenship of the People's Republic of China.

Persons included in the above-mentioned group, because they have only one citizenship, are not required to choose their citizenship under the provisions of the dual nationality treaty. If they so desire, a certificate stating their position may be given to such persons.[24] (Parenthesis in the original.)

When the text of the notes was released, this provision aroused a storm of comment and speculation as to who would or should be included among those paradoxical persons of dual nationality having only one nationality. Newspapers went to their "informed sources" and "sources near to the Cabinet" and found out that before the Prime Minister left for China the Cabinet had discussed this problem, probably at the insistence of the Minister of Health, Lie Kiat Teng, who flatly refused to submit himself to another option procedure. The sources agreed that it had been decided that Chinese-descent Cabinet Ministers, Members of Parliament, and members of the Police and Armed Forces would be released from the obligation of opting again. Beyond this, most sources agreed that all other government employees would also be exempted, while one source went so far as to mention all registered voters of Chinese descent.[25] None of these reports, however, was confirmed by the Government, and no further clarification was made.

Opponents of a new round of options immediately saw in this new provision the possibility of converting the active system of the treaty into a passive one. Referring to the words "in the opinion of the Government of the Republic of Indonesia" in Paragraph 2 of the notes, Siauw Giok

24 Unofficial translation from the Indonesian text
25 *Keng Po*, June 16, 1955, and *Sin Min*, May 27, 1955.

Tjhan maintained that this meant that China was giving the Indonesian Government complete freedom to determine who among the dual nationals should be considered to have Indonesian citizenship alone. He proposed that the Indonesian Parliament, when considering the bill, should pass an amendment stipulating that the definition of those who would automatically have only Indonesian citizenship without further option should be as wide as possible, so that it would, in practice, include all those who were already citizens under the passive system of the Round Table Agreement.[26]

A few days later the Indonesian Socialist Party (PSI) issued a statement incorporating the same suggestion. The Government must take this opportunity, it said, to declare that all persons of Chinese descent who are already citizens according to the Provisional Constitution should not be considered to have dual nationality and should therefore not be required to repudiate Chinese citizenship The statement closed with the assertion that "for only a certain group among those of Chinese descent (Ministers, Members of Parliament, etc.) to be freed from the obligation of opting again would be in poor taste and might be considered as an invitation to the leaders of the Peranakan community to sacrifice the fate of their group to their own personal interests."[27] This statement gained the support of the editors of the Semarang paper *Kuangpo*, and no doubt also of a majority of the former opponents of the treaty.

Ratification of the Treaty

Up to the time of its resignation on July 24, 1955, the Cabinet took no further action on the treaty or on the new issues raised by the exchange of notes. The new Cabinet which took office on August 8 was based on a coalition consisting almost entirely of parties which had opposed the treaty. With national parliamentary elections less than two months away, political parties were busy with campaigning, and the Government generally attended only to what might be considered "interim" affairs. Neither the Cabinet nor Parliament desired to initiate consideration of the Dual Citizenship Treaty until the formation of a new government on the basis of the newly elected Parliament.

In March 1956, the new cabinet was installed. Led by Ali Sastroamidjojo

---

26 *Keng Po*, June 16, 1955.
27 *Keng Po*, June 20, 1955.

of the PNI, it was a coalition which included several of the parties which had opposed the treaty. During June the Prime Minister put considerable effort into achieving, among the government parties, agreement on the treaty. He held a "working session" with the Foreign Affairs Section of Parliament but met strenuous opposition from representatives of the Catholic and Protestant parties. There were hints that strong pressure was being applied to the Catholic and Protestant members of the Cabinet; and considerable differences of opinion were evident among the leaders of these two parties.[28]

On July 3, the coalition cabinet finally endorsed the treaty. It was forwarded to Parliament as a draft bill in early August. A "clarification" attached to the bill reasserted Indonesia's right under the Ali-Chou notes to determine who should be exempted from the active option clause. Although it was not specifically so stated, it was generally understood that all those who had voted in national or local elections would be considered to have lost their Chinese citizenship and would not be required to opt again for Indonesian citizenship. Indeed, it is extremely unlikely that the Cabinet could have endorsed the treaty without this kind of compromise.

In December 1956, the Minister of Justice urged Parliament to ratify the treaty soon; but it was March 1957 before sectional meetings of the legislature began discussion of the matter. Meanwhile, the rebellion had broken out in Sumatra. The Cabinet was divided on the issues involved and was forced to resign. In April Parliament was recessed. About six weeks later it was reopened, after the extra-parliamentary cabinet of Djuanda had been installed. In August the new cabinet discussed and approved the treaty. In a report to the Central Committee of BAPERKI in October, Siauw Giok Tjhan blamed the changes of cabinet for Indonesia's long delay in ratifying the treaty.[29] A few weeks later, Foreign Minister Subandrio wrote to Parliament urging it to give high priority to the treaty.

The legislature finally debated ratification on November 21 and 25, 1957. The debate revolved around four points. One of these, the status of pro-Kuomintang Chinese whom the Government was treating as

---

28 *Republik*, June 20, 1956, and July 5, 1956.
29 *Republik*, October 21, 1957.

"stateless," will be discussed in Chapter VI because the treaty does not directly concern this group.

A second issue was raised by a Masjumi member, St. Mangkuto, who called for reconsideration (or, actually, rejection) of the treaty on the grounds that "recognition of Chinese as Indonesian citizens would endanger the Indonesian nation."[30] Accusing the Chinese of a propensity for illegal activities, he alleged that they were disrupting the economy.[31] Although there were undoubtedly many who sympathized with this position, no other legislator supported it openly. One Moslem representative (IPKI) protested against the speech as unworthy of a follower of Islam.

Most opponents of the treaty raised a different issue: they demanded that debate on the treaty be postponed until after Parliament had passed a bill on citizenship and naturalization. It was argued that Parliament might favor provisions in a citizenship law which were incompatible with the treaty. Support for this position came from the IPKI and PSI (Socialist Party), and the numerically strong Nahdatul Ulama (Religious Scholars Association). Anwar Harjono, claiming to speak for the Masjumi, also called for postponement. He said that the Masjumi had not yet determined its final stand on the treaty. In what appeared to be an indirect repudiation of the position taken by St. Mangkuto, he Stated that his party regretted that the treaty had been drawn up hastily without consultation with the people most concerned, Indonesia's citizens of Chinese descent.[32]

Deputy Prime Minister Hardi, in his capacity as Acting Foreign Minister, joined the debate twice to point out that there could be no contradiction between a dual citizenship treaty which concerns only those who already have citizenship and a citizenship law which applies only to those who do not yet have citizenship. Speaking for the Government, he insisted that Parliament deal with the treaty first.[33]

It is extremely doubtful whether the Government could have won a vote against postponement of debate on the treaty at this time. Speakers favoring postponement represented parties with a total of 133 votes in Parliament. Parties whose spokesmen had shown a willingness to deal with

30 *Sin Min*, November 23, 1957.
31 *Sin Min*, November 27, 1957.
32 *Republik*, November 22, 1957.
33 *Sin Po*, November 23, 1957.

the treaty before discussing a citizenship bill had a total of 97 votes. These figures are presented here only as a general indication of the strength of the opposition to ratification at this time. Actually, it cannot be assumed that those who took a stand on the issue always represented all members of their parties in Parliament. Furthermore, because of the conflict between the central government and the military commanders in the Outer Islands, many members were absent from Parliament. Thus it is impossible to say how an actual vote would have turned out. Nevertheless, it is clear that the Government felt constrained to make a concession regarding the postponement issue. The Cabinet quickly agreed upon a citizenship bill and submitted it to Parliament just a few days before debate on the treaty was scheduled to begin again. As was shown in the previous chapter, no party had serious objections to this new citizenship bill. Furthermore, no one found serious contradictions between it and the treaty. Thus it became difficult to argue that the citizenship bill should be passed first.

On December 17, 1957, the final debate on the treaty took place. Spokesmen for the Government, supported by Siauw Giok Tjhan of BAPERKI, urged immediate ratification. They argued that it was desirable to settle the matter of dual citizenship as soon as possible so that current government measures against alien Chinese would not be applied to citizen Chinese. A Masjumi motion to postpone debate until after the citizenship law had been passed was defeated by 39-110. The Masjumi and Socialist Party representatives then walked out, and the treaty was ratified by the unanimous vote of the remaining delegates.

It is clear that the question of postponing debate was not a real issue. The stand for postponement was taken by spokesmen of parties which had serious objections to the treaty itself or which could not agree among themselves The major issue was the type of option system to be used and the groups which should be exempted from making options. It was not until a compromise appeared to have been reached on this matter that several parties abandoned their demand for postponing debate. The developments surrounding the discussion of this issue will now be traced.

On November 9, 1957, before the treaty was debated by Parliament, the Government submitted a paper replying to questions which had been raised in the earlier sectional meetings. The paper stated that those to be exempted from active options would be those whose "social and political position" demonstrated that they had voluntarily relinquished Chinese citizenship. The following examples were given: those who have important roles in the political life of the nation, those who hold important positions in the Government or its agencies, and those who have often represented Indonesia abroad in cultural, sports, and other matters. The Government made it clear, however, that registration and voting were not to be taken as proof of citizenship permitting exemption from the option requirement.[34] This meant that the Djuanda Cabinet was not accepting the compromise which the previous cabinet had worked out between the PNI on one side and the Masjumi, Catholic, and Protestant parties on the other.

When debate opened on November 21, the Communist Party (PKI), BAPERKI, and the Catholic and Protestant parties demanded that the Government use its right under the Chou-Ali notes to pronounce all voters exempt from the option clause of the treaty, on the grounds that voting amounted to a voluntary rejection of Chinese citizenship. The Nahdatul Ulama was in favor of the treaty, but how its members stood on the exemption issue was not generally known. The Masjumi and the Socialist parties were opposed to any active option system. Thus the Nationalist Party (PNI) was the only major party which could be counted upon to support the treaty as presented by the Government.

Before the second round of debate, the Government made the minor concession of agreeing to include the Chou-Ali exchange of notes in the draft bill on the treaty. (Actually, the Government had announced earlier that this would be done.[35] At the end of the second day, however, Acting Foreign Minister Hardi reaffirmed the Government's intention not to exempt voters from opting. He said that since all citizens, including dual citizens, were registered voters, it would make the treaty meaningless to exempt voters.[36]

On December 5, Siauw Giok Tjhan and a group of thirteen other Chinese-descent leaders presented a petition to the Government. They urged that all "active" voters be considered to have only the citizenship of Indonesia, and that they therefore be exempt from options under the Dual Citizenship Treaty.[37] According to the press, the petitioners included all Chinese members of Parliament, the Constituent Assembly,

34 *Keng Po*, November 9, 1957, and *Antara*, November 10, 1957.
35 *Antara*, November 10, 1957.
36 *Sin Po*, November 23, 1957.
37 *Sin Po*, December 12, 1957.

and the National Council, with the sole exception of Tony Wen of the PNI.[38] On the delegation were representatives of the PNI, the PKI, BAPERKI, the Nahdatul Ulama, the Masjumi, and the Catholic Party, as well as three prominent non-party leaders. This was a striking demonstration of the united opposition of the Chinese community to active options.

A week later, Foreign Minister Subandrio asked Parliament to postpone discussion and action on the treaty, in order to allow the Government "to carry on discussions for achieving a practical and good settlement." The BAPERKI newspaper suggested that Tan Kiem Liong of the Nahdatul Ulama and Lie Poo Yoe of the PNI had been especially influential in gaining reconsideration of the issue by the Government.[39] Siauw Giok Tjhan and the other petitioners were invited to a conference with Dr. Subandrio soon afterwards.

On December 17, Parliament convened for its final debate on the treaty. Foreign Minister Subandrio opened the session with a statement on the option exemptions issue. According to one Chinese newspaper, he promised that the Government would "give very careful consideration to the possibility of accepting the suggestion of members of Parliament who urged that all voters of Indonesian citizenship and Chinese descent be considered to have only one citizenship, that is, Indonesian."[40]

It seems likely that this is almost exactly what Dr. Subandrio did say. But other pro-exemptions newspapers reported that he included voters in the list of groups which the Government promised, without qualification, to exempt from active options.[41] Apparently the members of Parliament who were opposed to active options and who favored the widest possible exemptions must also have understood that the Government had yielded to their position. As we have seen, the treaty was ratified unanimously and without debate as soon as the members of the Masjumi and Socialist parties had withdrawn. If the latter two parties had not been generally opposed to the Djuanda Cabinet, they might also have accepted the apparent compromise.

The Dual Citizenship Treaty was ratified by the Standing Committee

---

38 The text of the petition may be found in *Sin Min*, December 14, 1957.
39 *Republik*, December 13, 1957.
40 *Sin Po*, December 17, 1957.
41 *Keng Po*, December 17, 1957, and *Republik*, *Harian Rakjat*, and *Sin Min*, December 18, 1957.

of the National People's Congress of the People's Republic of China on December 30, 1957. Since only the formal exchange of ratifications in Peking was now required before the treaty would go into effect, it appeared that dual citizenship would soon be a thing of the past. But it was not until two years later that the exchange finally took place.

The delay was at least partly due to the fact that the issue of exemptions remained to be settled. In reply to a question from Siauw Giok Tjhan, Prime Minister Djuanda told Parliament at the end of January, 1958, that Subandrio had not promised to exempt voters; he had only said that the Government would consider the matter and would establish a committee to make recommendations.[42] About the same time, Subandrio affirmed that Chinese-descent members of Parliament might be appointed to this committee.[43] When it was finally established in April, however, the Interdepartmental Committee on Dual Citizenship did not include a single member of Chinese origin. Headed by Sudjono of the Foreign Ministry, it was made up of fifteen members representing the Foreign, Justice, Home Affairs, Information, and Defense Ministries, as well as the Immigration Department, the Attorney General, and the Police Department.

In view of the composition of the committee, it is not surprising that its recommendations, embodied a year later in a government regulation on implementation of the treaty, did not include exemption for voters. Thus, after five years of debate, deadlock, and unsuccessful compromise, the supporters of the active option system finally overcame the dogged opposition of the Chinese community and a major, if not a predominant, section of Parliament.

Conclusions about the Dual Citizenship Treaty

The failure of the treaty to gain the immediate approval of a majority in Parliament, the strength of the arguments put forward by its critics, the somewhat paradoxical way in which the exchange of notes attempted to compromise with the opposition, and the eventual by-passing of the opposition, should not lead us to minimize the positive aspects of the Dual Citizenship Treaty. The treaty is, indeed, a historic achievement.

---

42 *Sin Po*, January 30, 1958.
43 *Sin Min*, January 24, 1958.

For the first time, China has relinquished her traditional claim that all persons of Chinese descent remain Chinese citizens even when they acquire another citizenship. Following the precedent of this treaty, other countries with a Chinese minority, such as Burma, may also seek treaties with China. Chou En-lai practically invited them to do so in his 1955 statement on the treaty.[44]

The treaty is a success also in that the Indonesian Government, through careful diplomacy and protracted negotiation, was able to achieve virtually all of its aims. Most important of these was, of course, the elimination of the thorny legal and jurisdictional problem of dual nationality – a goal sought by all groups. In addition, the major procedures embodied in the treaty were those advocated by the Indonesian side. As one legal analyst has pointed out, the Chou-Ali exchange of notes even gave the Indonesian Government what amounted to unilateral power to abrogate the Chinese citizenship of any group of dual nationals.[45]

The treaty's system of active options has a number of advantages, both for the Government and for the Indonesian Chinese. Many Indonesian leaders, even in the opposition parties, have opposed a passive system partly because it would allow the uninformed, apathetic, and uncertain dual citizens to become solely Indonesian by default. They want assurance that those who remain Indonesian citizens do so deliberately, and they believe that an active rejection of Chinese citizenship is the least Indonesia might expect as a demonstration of loyalty. Although the importance of this argument is primarily in the area of subjective feelings, it may also have significant consequences. Native Indonesians will be more satisfied with an active option system. It will therefore probably improve the attitudes of government officials and the Indonesian public towards citizen Chinese. The latter, having actively rejected their Chinese citizenship, may actually receive more equalitarian treatment than they would have if they had acquired Indonesian citizenship passively. Under the treaty's active system, the Chinese who are indifferent to Indonesian citizenship will become foreigners. They will therefore be a more legitimate target for discriminatory measures.

Another advantage of the active system is that in the option procedure

---

44 See Appendix VII.
45 Ko Swan Sik, *De Meervoudige Nationaliteit*, Leiden, 1957, p. 306.

every Chinese will be provided with some sort of document certifying his chosen citizenship. This should end the "proof of citizenship" problem which has brought considerable confusion and frustration both to government officials and to Chinese-descent citizens. On the other hand, it appears likely that under any passive system (including the proposed exemption of voters) the problems of determining and proving citizenship, along with the discrimination which attended them, would have been extended for many years into the future.

Finally, in spite of the burden it places on the Courts (which must hear and register declarations) the active system provides a method of determining citizenship which is less complicated (and therefore less susceptible to injustice or corruption) than an alternative passive system.

Having examined the positive aspects of the treaty, we now turn to the arguments against it. It should be recognized, in the first place, that many of the objections raised against the treaty were either exaggerated or groundless. For instance, the treaty would not create a group of stateless or displaced persons. Those who became Chinese subjects by default would be no more stateless or displaced than the already large group of foreign Chinese in Indonesia. Then, too, the treaty was attacked by one of its critics because it allowed persons who had already chosen Chinese citizenship to have another opportunity of choosing. Other critics, however, attacked the bill on the grounds that it did not. Actually, since the group in question had already lost their Indonesian citizenship, they were not included among the dual nationals to whom the treaty gave the right of another option. This would seem reasonable.

As we have seen, one of the major arguments against the treaty was that its active system would "denationalize" a large groups of Peranakans who failed to make any choice. These would be the "little people," the workers and farmers and small shopkeepers, the illiterate and uninformed, the people who for generations had lived in the villages and byways of Indonesia. The opponents of the treaty estimated the size of this group as anywhere from a "majority" to 80% of the Peranakan community, and implied that all or most of them would lose their citizenship without their knowledge or consent.

The present writer believes this argument to be vastly overstated. Since the war years there has been a significant shift of the Chinese Population away from villages and into towns and cities. Today only a small proportion of Chinese live in localities where there are less than two hundred other Chinese. Even in small towns there is usually at least one Chinese community organization and often a school. And village Chinese almost invariably have extensive commercial, social, and family contacts with Chinese of larger centers. There are few Chinese families who do not have at least one literate member.

These facts suggest that even a moderate campaign, through posters, press, schools, and Chinese organizations, will reach the vast majority of Peranakans with the basic facts about the new opting period. The writer believes that among those who feel they have a stake in Indonesian citizenship, very few will fail to opt for it. There will be a small number who will do nothing. But we may assume that many of these will be persons who are knowingly taking the easiest way to acquire Chinese citizenship, and that most of the rest will be persons who, although not particularly interested in Chinese citizenship, at least know that they are acquiring it by their passivity. Thus it seems unlikely that the active system will result in a large group of people losing their Indonesian citizenship "unknowingly" or "unwillingly."

In early debates on the treaty, it was argued that to revoke any persons's Indonesian citizenship without his concurrence would be unconstitutional, even if he had another citizenship. This criticism appears to have been well founded, because the Provisional Constitution guaranteed that all persons who had acquired Indonesian citizenship would retain it at least until the promulgation of a new citizenship law.[46] The 1958 citizenship act specifically dealt with this problem by providing, in Section 17, that citizenship can be revoked for failing to reject a foreign citizenship when the person concerned has an opportunity of doing so.

A Masjumi member of Parliament maintained that it would be "detrimental to the nation" to allow freedom for a husband and wife of different nationalities to retain their separate citizenships.[47] Presumably this provision of the treaty was originally conceived in accordance with the principle of freedom of choice of citizenship. No doubt it was China which insisted that the treaty should assure the same rights to women as to men. In any case, the Indonesian citizenship act of 1958 provides that

---

46 See Appendix III.
47 *Sin Min*, November 27, 1957.

in the case of an alien woman marrying an Indonesian, she automatically acquires Indonesian citizenship unless her husband gives up his. On this point, then, the principles of freedom of choice and sexual equality which are embodied in the treaty have been modified in the citizenship law. Presumably common citizenship for husband and wife is a more importance principle to the Indonesian Government and Parliament. If a Chinese woman ever marries an Indonesian and both parties wish to keep their own citizenship, the Courts may have to decide which takes precedence, the treaty or the 1958 law. So far as the writer knows, this discrepancy was not mentioned in the Parliamentary debates on postponement.

The treaty does allow either partner in a marriage between a Chinese and an Indonesian to acquire voluntarily the citizenship of the other. But it contains no other provision for naturalization. In the concluding chapter of this report, the pros and cons of naturalization of Chinese aliens will be discussed. It will be seen that, from one point of view at least, the lack of a naturalization provision in the treaty may be considered to be a notable shortcoming.

Another objection to the treaty was the claim that its active option system would tend to alienate, rather than to attract, the Peranakan population. Spokesmen for virtually all sections of the Chinese community made it quite clear, in the press, in Parliament, and in public speeches, that they were opposed to active options. Official government policy has always been to attract and to assimilate Chinese-descent citizens. Because of the feelings of the Chinese, the active option system will jeopardize this policy, at least slightly. It was partly awareness of this fact which caused the Government to consider exempting various categories of Chinese from the option procedure. If all active voters had been exempted, the problem would have been overcome, because for the great majority of Chinese a passive system would have been in effect. The exemptions finally allowed by the Government apply, however, to only a relatively small number of Chinese.[48] This is likely to be regarded as unfair and unreasonable by the majority of Chinese, and perhaps even by many who are to be exempted.[49]

The Government maintained that to exempt all voters would make the

---

48 See Appendix VIII.
49 See, for instance, criticism by the lawyer, Ko Swan Sik, as reported in *Sin Po*, February 1, 1958.

treaty meaningless, since all citizens were registered voters. This position was logically sound. But Siauw Giok Tjhan replied that, in fact, a large number of citizens had not been registered, either because of their own indifference or because of discrimination or misunderstanding of the law on the part of registration officials. At this time, Siauw was asking that all registered electors be exempted; but later demands for exemptions included only "active voters." Siauw estimated that from 20% to 30% of citizen Chinese had not been registered.[50] While this seems an exaggerated figure, it is likely that at least this proportion failed to vote. Under any exemption procedure, then, the treaty would apply to a large number of Chinese.

There is no doubt that to exempt either registered electors or "active voters" would have involved many injustices and difficulties. In some areas (though not in most) many citizen Chinese had been left off the voters lists against their will. Fortuitous circumstances had caused others not to vote. These persons would therefore be considered dual citizens, while others with the same legal status would not. The writer believes, also, that either lists of electors or local records showing which electors voted would be a very difficult and unreliable basis for determining citizenship.

No doubt those who advocated exempting voters from options were aware of these problems. In the opinion of this writer, their position must be interpreted primarily as an attempt to suggest a compromise through which the Government might conceivably accept a modified passive system of options. As we have seen, however, the Government was determined to institute the active system.

In conclusion, we venture to suggest that in spite of delays and shortcomings in the way it was brought about, the implementation of the treaty will provide a reasonably successful solution to the problems of dual citizenship. Its effects on the Chinese minority problem in general will be evaluated in the final chapter.

---

50 *Republik*, December 4, 1957.

C H A P T E R   F I V E
DEMOGRAPHY OF CHINESE CITIZENSHIP

Immigration and Population

When the Dutch arrived in the Indies at the beginning of the seventeenth century, they found settlements of Chinese traders here and there throughout the islands. Under the rule of the Dutch East India Company the Chinese prospered, and their community grew fairly rapidly. During his administration of Java from 1811 to 1816, Sir Stamford Raffles estimated that there were nearly 100,000 Chinese in Java and Madura. By 1900 this number had increased to about 277,000, and in the following thirty years it more than doubled, reaching 582,000 in 1930. The Chinese population in the Outer Islands was increasing at an equally fast rate, and the total Chinese population for the Indies was enumerated at 1,233,000 in 1930, the year of the last complete census.[1]

Since Chinese women did not emigrate to the Indies in significant numbers until after World War I, the increase in the Chinese population was due partly to large-scale immigration, a major part of which was indentured plantation labor, and partly to the fact that from the beginning immigrants had taken Indonesian wives and raised their children as Chinese. Thus there came to exist two Chinese communities: the Totoks, or recent immigrants, and the Peranakans, who were born in Indonesia and were usually the children or the descendants of mixed marriages. Although the distinction between these two groups is based chiefly upon birthplace, the Indies-born children of Tokoks are often considered as Totoks if they continue to use the Chinese language and adhere to a distinctly Chinese way of life. Because most Peranakans have had at least one mixed-marriage among their ancestors, the name often bears the

---

1 Purcell, *op. cit.*, pp. 443 and 449.

connotation of "mixed-blood.. Roughly, however, the two terms may be used to distinguish China-born and Indies-born Chinese.

As we have seen, the Netherlands Citizenship Act of 1910 claimed as Dutch subjects all Chinese who were born in the Indies of domiciled parents. Thus the 1930 census figures for foreign-born and Indies-born Chinese give us an approximate idea not only of the numbers of Totoks and Peranakans, but also of foreigners and subjects. In that year there were about 750,000 Indies-born Chinese, and 450,000 Chinese immigrants.[2] This means that almost two-thirds of the Chinese living in the Indies were Dutch subjects.

Taking into account actual and probable immigration figures and birth and death rates, the writer estimates that there were some 2,100,000 Chinese in Indonesia in 1950, of whom about 1,500,000, or over 70%, were born there. The foreign-born Chinese population, according to the same estimate, was about 600,000. Since 1950 no significant amount of Chinese immigration into Indonesia has been permitted, and the percentage of Totoks, as compared with that of Peranakans, has been decreasing at the rate of about one per cent per year.

Options for Chinese Citizenship

A good deal of mystery surrounds the question of how many Chinese gave up their Indonesian citizenship during the option periods of 1946-48 and 1949-51. The present writer was unable to obtain any figures or reliable estimates of the results of the options under the Act of 1946. Final figures for the 1949-51 period have never been released, and probably never can be. The Courts in many areas were exceedingly slow in "processing" the declarations of repudiation of Indonesian citizenship which had been made before them. The Ministry of Justice finally ordered all such processing to cease on January 1, 1958. This meant that many cases of repudiation were never officially certified. For example, it was reported that in the municipality of Semarang from 500 to 1,000 such cases were suspended before final certification of alien citizenship was issued.[3]

Unofficial reports gave a wide range of estimates for the numbers of 1949-51 options. An officer of BAPERKI claimed that not more than 10%

---

2   *Ibid.*, p. 444.
3   *Sin Min*, Semarang, March 13, 1958.

of the Peranakan Community could have chosen Chinese citizenship. In reporting the preliminary negotiations between Indonesia and China concerning dual citizenship, the correspondent of the *Times of India* obtained the estimate in Peking that out of about 2,000,000 Chinese in Indonesia, only 800,000 were Indonesian citizens.[4] These figures must have been based on the assumption that from 35% to 40% of the Indonesian-born Chinese had rejected Indonesian citizenship or lost it through the rejections of their parents or husbands. Government sources in Indonesia, on the other hand, have given unofficial estimates of about 30%.

The Government published official lists of persons who had repudiated Indonesian citizenship, but these were far from complete. Up until 1954 they included only 24,192 Chinese names.[5] Unofficial repudiation figures for various localities appeared in the press, however. By comparing these with population statistics from various sources, the present writer estimates the following local percentages of Indonesian-born Chinese who repudiated their Indonesian citizenship: Djakarta 25%; Jogjakarta, 25%; Surakarta, 20%; and Semarang, 10%.[6]

Towards the end of 1954, all foreigners residing in Indonesia were registered by local immigration authorities. By subtracting our estimate of the number of foreign born Chinese living in Indonesia in 1954 from the approximate number of foreign Chinese registered in that year, we calculate that the number of Chinese who had lost Indonesian citizenship through repudiations must have been between 250,000 and 350,000. Thus the proportion of Peranakans who chose Chinese citizenship in the 1949-51 option period was most probably between 17% and 25%. And, if our estimates are correct, from 40% to 45% of the Chinese living in Indonesia in 1955 were considered Chinese subjects. Whether the new round of options called for in the Dual Citizenship Treaty will substantially change this picture is a matter for speculation. But it appears that, under any circumstances except mass deportation, there will soon be at least one million alien Chinese in Indonesia.

---

4 *Sin Min*, Semarang, December 4, 1954.
5 From an unpublished study on Indonesian citizenship by H. van Marle.
6 These estimates are based upon figures from various newspaper and government reports and from van Marle's unpublished study. They probably include many unnecessary or illegal repudiations, since the regulations were often misunderstood or misinterpreted.

There were a little over 300 Chinese in all Indonesia who, in rejecting Indonesian citizenship in the 1949-51 option period, chose to remain Netherlands subjects rather than Chinese subjects.[7]

In closing, the writer would like to emphasize that almost all of the figures given in this section are subject to substantial error, either because they are based partly on guesses or because the original methods of enumeration were far from precise.

---

7   From van Marie's unpublished study.

THE POSITION OF FOREIGN CHINESE IN INDONESIA

In a series of clauses based on the United Nations' Universal Declaration of Human Rights, the 1950 Provisional Constitution of the Republic of Indonesia guaranteed to all persons living in Indonesia, including foreigners, a wide measure of rights and freedoms. Article 8, for instance, provided that "all persons within the territory of the State are entitled to equal protection of person and property," and other provisions guaranteed fundamental legal rights, freedom of movement and residence, freedom of opinion and expression, the right to join trade unions and to strike, and equal protection against any discrimination. Article 33 allowed limitation of these rights only by laws "exclusively for the purpose of securing the indispensable recognition and respect for the rights and freedoms of others and to comply with the just requirements of public order, morality, and welfare in a democratic community."

The activities of alien Chinese were subject to very little supervision or control before 1954. As the internal situation worsened, government and public suspicion and distrust of the Chinese deepened. Control measures were instituted as fast as they could be enforced, or perhaps faster. There were both political and economic reasons; for this. Pro-Peking Chinese were distrusted by government and army officials who disliked the Communist ideas and loyalties which were being spread by the political activists among them. On the other hand, pro-Kuomintang Chinese were accused of activities detrimental to the state. And when the press began to report that the Sumatra rebels were obtaining aid from Taiwan, there was a great popular outcry. Many organizations passed resolutions urging the Government to take more and more drastic measures against the local pro-Kuomintang Chinese. In addition, there had always been a widespread desire to curb the economic strength of the Chinese, especially of the alien Chinese.

Alien Control Measures

New immigration laws, passed in 1950, virtually prohibited any further Chinese immigration. Only a token quota, and persons invited by the Government, such as technicians, were to be admitted. Nevertheless, it is generally believed that clandestine immigration, especially of well-to-do pro-Kuomintang refugees, continued in fairly large numbers. Not a few such persons have been discovered and deported.

Partly as a check on illegal immigrants, and partly as a means of closer supervision over all foreigners, Alien Control Regulation PP45 was promulgated by the Government in 1954. This established an Alien Control Bureau under the Police Department. All foreigners were required to register with local branches of this bureau within a certain period. The regulation included also the following provisions for the supervision of the movements of aliens: upon changing residence, a foreigner must report to the police and receive from them an official letter which he must submit to the police at his new place of residence; upon moving, a foreigner must also report to the nearest Immigration Office, and to the civil authorities at both his old and new residences; upon travelling outside his place of residence for more than thirty days, a foreigner must report to the police and receive a travel certificate; hotels must keep a separate register for alien guests, and must require aliens to fill out two copies of report forms, which are to be submitted to the police daily; anyone entertaining a foreigner (whether a member of the family or not) in his home for one or more nights must report to the police within twenty-four hours.

This regulation was not strictly enforced at first. A police authority stated in 1956 that there had been about thirty violations per month in Djakarta alone.[8] Enforcement became more and more stringent. Heavy fines and jail sentences were imposed upon offending aliens in various cities from time to time.

Another 1954 measure was the Alien Registration Regulation PP32, which required that all aliens register with the nearest Immigration Offices,

---

8   *Sin Po*, May 29, 1956.

and thereafter report all births, deaths, marriages, divorces, changes of occupation, and changes of address to the same office. In the following year, a provisional law required immigrants to renew their Entrance Permits at fixed intervals during a period of fifteen years, whereupon they must apply for a Permanent Residence Permit. A foreigner who had been in the country for fifteen years or more was required to obtain a Certificate of Residence from the Justice Department, after payment of a fee of 500 rupiahs (over $40), plus 300 rupiahs for his wife and for each child. This amounted to a rather stiff head tax on the foreign population.

Beyond these general controls, the Government was determined to keep foreigners from taking part in, or trying to influence Indonesian politics. In this connection, any action or attitude which is related to the "life of the state," or which is intended to influence it is considered to be political.[9] The Constitution reserves for citizens the right to take part in government, and it allows the Government to restrict the freedoms of foreigners (or citizens) in the interests of the security or welfare of the state. Government authorities have repeatedly warned aliens to refrain from all political activity.

Considering the strong political currents in the Chinese community and their potential effect, not only upon Indonesian citizens of Chinese descent, but also upon the nation as a whole, the Government endeavored to curb political activities in the Chinese community. Restrictions fell most heavily upon Kuomintang supporters. First their traditional annual celebrations on October 10, and other such public activities, were forbidden. In 1958, all Kuomintang organizations, including youth groups and scout troops, were banned. Later schools and businesses with Kuomintang connections were closed, and many of these were seized or confiscated.

In October 1954, the Justice Department deported four prominent Kuomintang Chinese on the grounds that their activities were endangering the welfare of the nation. The exact charges against these men were not made public. Government opponents charged that corruption was involved, while Government supporters alleged that the deported persons had been involved in a plot to oust the Government parties and force the resignation of the President. Either or both of these explanations may have had some basis in reality, but it seems equally plausible that

---

9 Soenario, *op. cit.*, p. 19.

the Government's action was at least in part due to the fact that leading Kuomintang businessmen had cornered the rubber market in order to prevent the sale of rubber to Communist China under the terms of the Indonesia-China trade agreement.

About the same time that the Justice Department was moving against Kuomintang leaders, the Military Police arrested three leftist Chinese. As a result of these moves, alien Chinese, especially on the Kuomintang side, became much more cautious about indicating their political orientation in public. Nevertheless, deportations have continued.

Alien Press Control

In 1952, a special department of the Ministry of Education was established to regulate and supervise foreign schools, most of which were Chinese. In trying to eliminate political teachings, it issues periodic lists of proscribed books and texts which may not be used in Chinese schools. Similarly, the Attorney General periodically issues regulations banning the import or circulation of certain foreign books.

In April 1958, a military decree banned the publication or circulation of any newspapers or magazines in the Chinese language. Thirty-four Chinese newspapers, including five in Djakarta, were forced to close. The reason given was that the military authorities responsible for national security could not obtain personnel capable of continuous inspection and supervision of Chinese publications.[10] In May, the regulation was modified to allow publication of selected Chinese-language papers under close military supervision. A preamble explained that this was to enable the Government to reach Chinese-language readers with its information and opinions.[11] By December, eleven Chinese newspapers were being published under these conditions.

Control of Foreign Schools

After it was established in 1952, the Inspectorate of Foreign Education of the Ministry of Education exercised increasing supervision and control over Chinese-language schools. Textbooks and curricula were carefully regulated. In 1957, all principals and teachers in foreign-language schools

---

10 *Sin Po*, April 18, 1958.
11 *Sin Po*, May 24, 1958.

were required to take examinations in the Indonesian language.

In March 1957, when the President declared a "state of siege" in the country, military authorities were given supreme power. Thus Djuanda had greater authority as Minister of Defense than he had as Prime Minister. In November 1957, after military commanders in some areas had already taken the initiative in closing Chinese schools, Djuanda issued a military regulation decreeing sweeping changes in foreign education. Foreign-language schools were to be severely limited in number, and those remaining were to be even more strictly regulated and supervised. All Indonesian citizens were to be transferred into Indonesian-language schools which followed the national curriculum. The decree left details of implementation to the Ministry of Education.

Subsequent regulations allowed foreign schools to be maintained in only the major cities and a handful of towns in each province, about 150 places in all. Within six months the number of Chinese-language schools had been reduced from over one thousand to a few hundred.

The 1957 Alien Tax

In July 1957, the Government announced a head tax for foreigners: 1500 rupiahs for each alien family head, and somewhat less for wives and children (regardless of citizenship). The amount of the tax was clearly exorbitant. It could not be paid without serious hardship, except by a minority of wealthy aliens. The Chinese ambassador and Chinese consuls in many cities called on government officials to request reconsideration. Chinese organizations in at least two dozen cities and towns sent petitions or delegations to government authorities. Several leaders of BAPERKI and the PKI (Communist Party) openly opposed the tax. A dozen or more suicides were attributed to the tax, in spite of newspaper opposition to this way of dealing with the problem!

As a result of these various forms of pressure, the Government finally announced that the tax could be paid in installments, or that, in the case of the really poor, applications for reduction of the tax or complete exemption might be made. No doubt the government tax offices were flooded with such applications. Chinese organizations in a great many towns and cities assisted aliens in filling out the required exemption forms. Some of the applications were granted, but many were not. The Chinese press reported that in some localities no exemptions or reductions were allowed.[12] Since the Provisional Constitution gives tax-levying powers only to Parliament, the Government submitted the alien tax decree as draft legislation in June 1958. The PKI (Communist Party) and several minor parties opposed the bill, calling for a progressive tax instead. Nevertheless, the bill was passed the following month.

Restrictions on the Economic Activities of Alien Chinese

In the economic sphere, the first move of the Government was to put an end to the remittances which Chinese had been sending to their families in Chin. This policy was in part dictated by economic necessities. Because of the difficult economic position of Indonesia after the war years, the supply of foreign exchange was very limited, and the Government had to insist that all available credit in foreign currencies should be utilized in ways beneficial to the home economy. In addition, the prohibiting of remittances to China was based upon the understandable conviction that the profits made by foreign businessmen in Indonesia should be spent or invested in Indonesia, and not transferred abroad.

Under each successive cabinet, policies concerning the economic position of the Chinese were different in detail and degree of effectiveness. But all were based upon the desire to build up an Indonesian middle class which would come to have a position of economic welfare and power equal to or greater than that of the Chinese. Under Iskaq Tjokrohadisurjo, Minister of Economic Affairs in the first Ali Sastroamidjojo Cabinet, this policy was implemented with more stringent regulations than ever before.

In the first place, foreign credit was available to businessmen only through the Ministry of Economic Affairs, and Iskaq extended the privileges accorded to Indonesians, as opposed to Chinese, in this field. Foreign exchange is of crucial importance to almost all large-scale business enterprises in Indonesia because it is the only medium for the procurement of goods from abroad-either capital goods to equip and maintain productive enterprises, or consumer goods for sale to the general public. Thus control over the allocation of foreign credit gave the Government wide powers over the fate of the various sectors, of the

---

12 *Hsin Pao*, October 11, 1957, and *Sin Po*, January 29, 1958.

business community. Iskaq announced that concerns owned by aliens would receive only 15% of the available foreign exchange, and that only by turning over 50% of their capital and profits to native Indonesian business partners could foreign Chinese firms avoid this limitation. This represented a drastic reduction in the opportunities open to foreign Chinese capital, which had hitherto played a dominant role in handling imports from other Asian nations.

The second means of reducing the importance of foreign Chinese in the economy was to exclude them from certain lines of activity. Previous cabinets had outlined certain economic activities which would be reserved for government development alone, and others that would be reserved for citizens. However, no serious steps had been taken to oust foreign Chinese from fields in which they were already entrenched.

Under Iskaq, the policy of excluding foreign Chinese from important new fields was continued. For instance, in its program to establish new industries with imported machines, equipment, and technical aid, the Government invited the participation only of citizens and foreigners having "national capital." The term "national capital" was not concretely defined, and the federation of the Chinese Sianghwee organizations proposed that all Chinese capital be included, since none of the profits of Chinese capital could be transferred abroad. In practice, however, the term was interpreted to exclude most foreign Chinese. In Central Java, for instance, government aid in establishing industries was confined entirely to citizens, and alien Chinese businessmen could obtain no foreign credits for this purpose.

Iskaq's policy was extended also to the exclusion of foreign Chinese from lines of business where they were already active. In 1954 and 1955 licenses for the importation of textiles were granted only to concerns or combines owned wholly or mostly by citizens. This left a great many Chinese textile wholesalers with empty shelves. By Government Regulations PP42 and PP60 of 1954, foreigners were forbidden to own or even to hold shares in rice mills. This meant that about a dozen large rice mills owned by alien Chinese in Central Java, and an even greater number in East Java and elsewhere, had to be sold or rented to "national" concerns, while many foreign Chinese had to sell their individual interests in a good many others.

As a result of these and similar measures, there was a considerable slump in the business activity of the foreign Chinese. A certain number of aliens re invested their capital in small-scale manufacturing not requiring equipment from abroad, in the building of theaters, hotels, and residences, and in the handling, processing and trading of local products. Others adopted a wait-and-see attitude, while putting their capital into real estate, Jewelry, gold, and other non-productive savings. Some accepted native Indonesian business partners, at least in name. A regrettably large number, however, were able to find either officials who could be bribed not to apply the restricting regulation in particular cases, or Indonesian "briefcase importers" whose sole business was to get import licenses from the Government and sell them (illegally) to foreign firms who could not get them otherwise. It was widely known that many party leaders and members of Parliament were engaged in such "national" enterprises. The extent of this kind of corruption and manipulation was a serious limitation on the effectiveness of the whole policy.

In September 1957, the Ministers of Industry and Trade issued a joint decree requiring all alien industries, trading companies, wholesalers, and retailers to register and to submit applications for licenses to continue operations. "Alien" enterprises were to include all businesses owned wholly or partly by aliens. In this regulation and subsequent ones, it was made clear that the Government intended to move gradually towards the exclusion of aliens from all lines of business. As a beginning, aliens were forbidden to establish any new enterprises, or to move or expand existing ones. In 1958, Parliament passed a bill which closed most types of small industry to aliens and set up a Foreign Capital Investment Council empowered to draw up lists of specifically excluded areas. The bill did guarantee, however, that in certain fields, such as plantations and major industries, foreign enterprises would not be excluded for at least twenty or thirty years.

In January 1958, a law concerning the employment of foreign personnel was promulgated. All employers of aliens were required to register their names, to give exhaustive details about them and their work, to pay 50 rupiahs for each, to request permission to continue employing them, and to report what had been done to train Indonesian citizens to take their places and what plans had been made for such replacement. Permits to employ foreign personnel had to be renewed in July 1958, and also whenever a change in position or type of work was to occur. Needless to say, the effect of this law was to discourage the employment of aliens. It may be used at any time to eliminate foreign workers from any type of employment.

THE POSITION OF INDONESIAN CITIZENS OF CHINESE DESCENT

Government Policy Towards Chinese-Descent Citizens

In its Political Manifesto of November 1, 1945, the Government of the Republic of Indonesia declared:

> In our internal policy we intend to implement the sovereignty of our people by putting into effect citizenship regulations which will in the shortest possible time encourage all groups of European and foreign Asian descent to become true Indonesians, that is, Indonesians who love democracy and their native country.[1]

These words are continually quoted on all Sides as the foundation of Indonesia's policy towards her foreign-descent minorities. It is generally agreed that the only way to achieve this aim is to treat minorities with absolute equality and without discrimination, and thus to encourage them to accept Indonesia wholeheartedly as their own country. The term "homogeneous" has been universally adopted to epitomize the kind of nation and society that should be striven for as an ideal.

In recent years the Government has interpreted these broad principles to mean that the Chinese minority should be completely assimilated into the general population, not only legally, but socially, psychologically, and culturally as well. It is hoped that the Chinese can gradually be led to drop all of their distinguishing characteristics and thus to become one with the majority group in thought, word, and deed. In this "melting pot" process, Indonesian society and culture would be enriched by contributions from

---

1 Unofficial translation.

the Chinese, but ultimately persons of Chinese descent would be no more characteristically Chinese than the rest of the population.

Successive Governments have repeatedly assured citizens of Chinese descent that there would be no discrimination against them – no distinctions between "indigenous" and "non-indigenous" citizens. In parliamentary debate on the Dual Citizenship Treaty, Siauw Giok Tjhan called upon the Government to make clear the consequences of choosing Indonesian citizenship, and especially to guarantee that discrimination would cease. About two weeks later, the Minister of Justice repeated the Government's promise that there would be no discrimination against citizens of foreign descent.[2]

President Soekarno and Vice-President Hatta have stood consistently against racial discrimination. Even when anti-Chinese feeling was running high, they publicly opposed any measures against "non-indigenous" citizens.[3]

Briefly stated, then, official policy towards citizen Chinese, as towards other minorities, has always been: assimilation without discrimination. In order to implement and develop this policy, and to advise and instruct various government departments and agencies in related matters, a Bureau of Minority and Alien Affairs was established in the Ministry of Home Affairs. This agency was known by its initials, UPBA. It had separate sections for the Arab, Eurasian, and Chinese minorities. Its organization suggested to many citizen Chinese that they were to be treated more as Chinese aliens than as citizens. Eventually, however, the supervision and control of aliens was removed from the jurisdiction of UPBA, and the name was changed to the Bureau of Minority Affairs.

As was shown in Chapter I, the relations which developed between Chinese and Indonesians in the colonial period resulted in considerable suspicion, prejudice, and differing interests between the two groups. Under these circumstances, the policy of assimilation was exceedingly difficult to implement. The transfer of all citizen Chinese children to national schools, which will be discussed below, was a major step towards assimilation. Another move in this direction was made by the Army Chief of Staff, General Nasution, in April 1958. In a proclamation to

---

2   *Sin Po*, December 12, 1957.
3   For instance, see *Republik*, October 21, 1957, and *Star Weekly*, No. 553, August 4, 1956.

citizens of foreign descent, he urged them not to mix with aliens, but to ally themselves with native Indonesian groups and organizations.[4] This accelerated the process of organizational separation which had been going on between the citizens and the foreigners among the Chinese.

We shall now examine various other Government regulations and measures affecting the citizen Chinese.

Legal and Political Position of the Citizen Chinese

Citizens of Chinese descent have, of course, the freedoms and rights which we have cited in the previous section as prerogatives of alien Chinese, in addition to all other rights guaranteed by the Provisional Constitution to the citizenry in general. Like other citizens, they are entitled to take part in government, and have the right to work and to receive an education. Article 25 provided that "the authorities shall not attach any advantages or disadvantages to the fact that citizens belong to a particular group of the population," while Article 7 stated that "all are entitled to equal protection against any discrimination and against the incitement to such discrimination."[5] Finally, Article 58 guaranteed that the Chinese minority shall have at least nine seats in the House of Representatives, and that this quota shall be made up by appointment if not attained by election. Representation was likewise guaranteed in the Constituent Assembly.

In the national elections of 1955, many parties included Chinese in their lists of candidates. In most areas of the country there was little or no discrimination in the registration of citizen Chinese electors. It appears that most Chinese voters supported BAPERKI, a Peranakan political organization. In the September elections, BAPERKI obtained almost 180,000 votes – sufficient to elect one representative, Siauw Giok Tjhan, to the Legislature. A Chinese candidate of the Communist Party (PKI) also won a seat. In the December election, several Chinese were elected to the Constituent Assembly.

In August 1956, the Government appointed seven Chinese to the Legislature, in order to meet the constitutional guarantee for minority representation. All but one of these were members of Government parties. Siauw Giok Tjhan, speaking for BAPERKI and its supporters,

---

4   *Sin Po*, April 17, 1958.
5   Official translation.

protested against these appointments. Pointing out that the election law required appointments to be made in accordance with the desires of the minority to be represented, he argued that this requirement could not be fulfilled by the appointment of obscure members of parties which had not received Chinese electoral support. The twelve Chinese who were appointed seven months later to the Constituent Assembly were chosen on a more non-partisan basis.

Proof of Citizenship

As a result of the historic division and prejudices between the Indonesians and Chinese, citizens of Chinese descent were frequently not accorded equal treatment with other citizens after the establishment of the Republic. Totoks and Peranakans alike were considered as undesirable aliens by many people, even by government officials, and regulations intended for foreigners were often applied to citizens of Chinese descent. Partly as a solution to this problem, the Ministry of Home Affairs decided to hold a general registration of all citizens of foreign descent, and to issue to each one a certificate of citizenship which could be shown in support of a claim to any of the rights of a citizen. A few days after this intention was announced, the Minister of Justice wrote a letter to the Minister of Home Affairs in which he maintained that for a government department to institute such a registration without an act of parliament was unlawful,[6] Various Peranakan spokesmen also raised serious objections to the proposed registration. The head of the Bureau of Minority and Alien Affairs (UPBA) then made a public statement in which he maintained that the jurisdictional competence of his Ministry in this matter was quite properly derived from the Round Table Agreements ratified by Parliament, and from the practice of the former Dutch regime. But he also announced that the plan would be withdrawn, and that the proposed certificates of citizenship would be issued only to those who requested them.[7]

Very few Chinese requested them. In Central Java, which has a Peranakan population of over 150,000, only 8,884 certificates were issued in almost two years. BAPERKI took a strong stand against the certificates.

---

6 *Berita BAPERKI*, Djakarta, Vol. I, No. 3, June 26, 1954, p. 4.
7 Soewahjo Soemodilogo, *Sedikit tentang So'al "Tanda Warga Negara,"* (statement issued by the Bureau of Minority Affairs), Djakarta, January 15, 1953.

Claiming that they had no legal foundation and that they represented a form of discrimination which would increase the "minority complex" of citizens of Chinese descent, BAPERKI spokesmen declared that they would only make the minority problem even more difficult to solve.[8] In a series of parliamentary questions to the Ministers of Justice and Home Affairs, Siauw Giok Tjhan asked why they should not be abolished altogether.[9]

Although officials of UPBA made it clear that citizens of foreign descent were not required to obtain citizenship certificates, various agencies in both central and local government began to demand them as proof of citizenship. Chinese who did not have such certificates were often treated as foreigners.

Many hotels, wary of the strict provisions of the Alien Control Act, refused accommodation to Chinese unless they could show either a foreign passport or the citizenship certificate. The Immigration Department in Surabaja, the Police in Wonosobo, and local officials in certain other places undertook to register as aliens all Chinese, including professed citizens, who did not have these certificates. Immigration offices also required the certificate, among other documents, from Chinese requesting passports.

Chinese who applied to government offices for various permits and privileges, such as foreign credit or recognition as "national enterprises," were often refused unless they could show a citizenship certificate. And in a few localities, in spite of specific instructions to the contrary, the committee in charge of registering qualified voters refused to register Chinese who could not show the certificate.

Many of the misapplications of the regulations were rectified. Specific instructions were sent out from Djakarta and other headquarters of assure that no citizens were registered as aliens. Officials of UPBA informed various agencies that the certificate of citizenship should not be required, but that other documents would suffice, such as a birth certificate plus a letter from the appropriate Court of Justice affirming that the bearer had not rejected Indonesian citizenship.

Nevertheless, each rectification was made only after BAPERKI leaders or other Peranakan spokesmen investigated cases and took specific

8 *Berita BAPERKI*, Djakarta, Vol. I, Nos. 7/8, October-November, 1954, p. 4.
9 *Ibid.*

complaints to the proper authorities. This reinforced the impression of many citizens of Chinese descent that it would always be necessary to struggle for their rights as citizens – an attitude which is not conducive to harmonious minority-majority relations. This negative result was often mentioned by opponents of the citizenship certificates. They also pointed out that the proof-of-citizenship system was a major source of corruption and "demoralization" of public officials at many levels. Bribes could be used either to obtain the certificates or to persuade officials not to demand them.

Possibly with such considerations as these in mind, the preelection interim cabinet of Burhanuddin Harahap established a committee to examine the citizenship certificate question. On the recommendation of this committee, the Minister of Home Affairs decreed that no further certificates would be issued after March 1, 1956. This regulation was distributed to officials in various departments in all parts of Indonesia.

At first this appeared to be a victory for the opponents of the proof-of-citizenship system. It soon became apparent, however, that the problem was not solved. Many government agencies continued to require citizenship certificates before granting licenses or other privileges. The head of UPBA for Central Java explained that the Government had not "abolished" the certificates, nor had it decided not to require them - it had merely stopped issuing them. Thus, for about a year, citizenship certificates were unobtainable but often required.

The legal basis for demanding the UPBA certificates was finally eliminated by the citizenship decree of June 4, 1957, issued by the Army Chief of Staff. This provided that:

Whoever is required by an official agency to prove whether he is a citizen or a foreigner must request the District Court at his place of residence to decide whether he is a citizen or not according to usual procedures.[10]

In an appended "explanation," the decree further stated that:

In order that the District Courts will not be flooded with requests

---

10 Unofficial translation.

to determine citizenship, the responsibility of the District Courts to determine citizenship is limited to those persons required to prove their Indonesian citizenship by an official agency.[11]

Thus UPBA citizenship certificates were superceded by court citizenship certificates. District Courts in the larger cities had to assign special judges to citizenship affairs. In the smaller cities and towns too, many Chinese applied for the new certificates.

A second military decree, announced by the Minister of Defense in August 1957, required very high fees for the court citizenship certificates: 1,000 rupiahs for adults, 500 rupiahs for each child, and 750 rupiahs for foreign women who married Indonesian citizens after December 1949. Because the decree was retroactive, those who had already obtained court certificates were also required to pay the fee. Exemption from payment was to be granted to those "clearly" unable to pay.

As was to be expected, the new regulation aroused strong protests from the citizen Chinese community. Since fees for various other licenses and permits were relatively low - a passport, for instance, required only 15 rupiahs - and since the Government had justified the fee on the grounds that the current national emergency required increased revenues, the "fee" appeared to be an exorbitant tax. Furthermore, the fee was announced shortly after a similarly heavy head tax had been levied against foreigners (mostly Chinese), and it therefore appeared that the Government was attempting to tax a racial (ethnic) group in a discriminatory manner. Finally, it was pointed out that even under emergency conditions, the Government had no constitutional power to levy taxes without parliamentary assent.

At the end of August, Siauw Giok Tjhan met with Prime Minister Djuanda to discuss the fee. Afterwards Siauw announced that an "understanding" had been reached. According to him, Djuanda had stated that the court certificate would be required only of those whose citizenship was in real doubt, and that proof of having participated in the national elections would ordinarily be considered sufficient proof of citizenship. Djuanda had assured Siauw that the regulation had no discriminatory intent whatsoever, since it could be applied also to "those

11 Unofficial translation.

who are usually called native" if their citizenship were in doubt. He had also maintained that the fee was never intended as a method of raising money, and had promised to correct those aspects of the regulation which suggested it. Presumably this referred to the statement in the preamble which mentioned the need for revenue, and possibly also to the fact that a man had to pay a fee for his wife and each of his children, even though their citizenship would not be in question.[12]

The Government appointed a committee to study the fee regulation. It was a month and a half before a revision was ready for publication. In the meantime, confusion and misapplications of the regulation occurred widely. For instance, newspapers reported that all citizen Chinese in the transport business in West Java were required to obtain court certificates within thirty days, and Chinese applying for or renewing driving licenses in Malang likewise had to show the certificates. In Djakarta, between ten and twenty citizen Chinese were served with alien tax notices; it was reported that they could only avoid the tax by showing court certificates which would cost almost as much to obtain. Another newspaper reported the case of a Chinese who possessed proof of not having rejected Indonesian citizenship, who had voted in the national elections, and who had been issued an Indonesian passport; when he applied for renewal of his passport, he was told that he must show the new court certificate. A duly elected Chinese representative in a district council was not admitted to his seat because he "could not show adequate proof of citizenship."

On October 10, 1957, the revised fee regulation was issued. It established a complicated procedure for obtaining the citizenship certificate - one in which the applicant had to appear before four different government officials. The fee was still to be 1,000 rupiahs, but there was no mention of fees for wives and children. Those unable to pay were required to provide supporting statements from a local civil servant and a local finance inspector. They also had to register their inability to pay with the clerk of the court. If at any time within five years their economic situation should improve, they would have to pay the fee.

The new regulation repeated the stipulation that the court certificate could only be required in cases of real doubt. It did not specify, however, what documents might be considered to prove citizenship beyond doubt.

---

12 *Sin Po* and *Keng Po*, August 31, 1957.

The Third Deputy Prime Minister later announced that each agency might establish its own requirements, and that proof of having participated in the elections would not necessarily be sufficient.[13] Later still, Djuanda, the Prime Minister, stated that a valid passport would "generally" be considered sufficient proof of citizenship, but that a certificate of not having rejected Indonesian citizenship would not.[14] The latter document, issued by local Courts of Justice, had been recognized by the Ministry of Education as the only valid proof.

The October revised regulation contained one provision which was welcomed by the Chinese. It specified that no government agency could require proof of citizenship unless it was enforcing regulations which distinguished between citizens and foreigners. Another provision allowed a person possessing legal proof of citizenship to have it investigated and validated by the District Court - without payment of the high fee. Thus court certificates or other court validated proofs continued to be necessary in obtaining various licenses and permits not available to aliens, but they were not legally required in other official matters, such as applying for driving licences.

In March 1958, all military decrees issued under the "state of emergency" expired. The June 1957 decree placing the responsibility for determining citizenship with the courts was renewed, but the August and October decrees which established exorbitant fees for the court certificates were not. Thereafter only a fee of sixty rupiahs, to cover court expenses, was required.

In view of the history of this contentious proof-of-citizenship issue, it seems likely that there will be no satisfactory solution until every Chinese has received a certificate Showing his declared citizenship under the provisions of the Dual Citizenship Treaty with China. Even then, many citizen Chinese will continue to resent having to show certificates which are not expected of other citizens.

Education of Citizens of Chinese Descent

Although no exact figures are available, it appears that in the early 1950's more than one-half of the children of Peranakans went to Chinese-

13 *Sin Po*, October 28, 1957.
14 *Keng Po*, January 30, 1958.

language schools, another large fraction went to Catholic and Protestant schools, and only a minority attended government schools. This meant that the segregated school system established by the Dutch and even more strongly enforced by the Japanese had been continued to a large extent in the post-war period.

This situation was considered highly undesirable by the Government. In the Chinese schools the pupils did study the Indonesian language, but they spent more time on Chinese. History, geography, and social studied were concerned more often with China than with Indonesia. Furthermore, the friendships, attitudes, and loyalties which a child developed in Chinese-language schools were not conducive to good Indonesian citizenship. Government authorities, therefore, repeatedly declared that it was not fitting for citizens to attend foreign schools, and one of the duties of the Inspectorate of Education for Foreigners was to encourage the transfer of Chinese Indonesian citizens to government schools. However, there was little incentive to push this program, because, in spite of remarkable progress in the expansion of the public school system, the number of government schools was far from adequate even to fulfill the needs of the indigenous population.

As another approach to this problem, the Department of Education established several Experimental Elementary Schools especially for Indonesian citizens of foreign descent. In schools of this kind for the children of Peranakans, the Chinese language was taught as a second language, and courses included material on Chinese history and culture. While this must be viewed as a positive and constructive step forward, it did not provide an adequate solution to the problem of education for citizen Chinese. There were never enough such schools to accommodate more than a minute fraction of Peranakan children, and insufficient financial resources made it difficult to assure a standard of teaching equal to that in many Chinese schools. There was also the theoretical objection that although the schools provided a "national education," they could contribute little towards assimilation as long as they remained segregated.

The issue of Chinese education was dramatically brought into the open in July of 1954, when the Djakarta Municipal Council unanimously passed a resolution urging the Government to prohibit Indonesian citizens from attending foreign schools and to convert foreign schools to national schools in cases where the proportion of pupils of Indonesian citizenship exceeded 25%. The originator of this motion was Takdir Alisjahbana, an outstanding literary figure and a member of the Socialist Party (PSI). In presenting his motion, he stated that some 200,000 Indonesian citizens of Chinese descent were attending foreign schools, and emphasized the disadvantages to Indonesia of this system.

This event created considerable consternation in the Peranakan community, partly because most of them opposed the substance of the motion, but also because they feared that it would give a false or prejudicial impression of their position. It might commonly be deduced, for instance, that Peranakans are, as a group, more loyal to China than to Indonesia. The fact that a large number of Peranakan children (perhaps as many as 50,000)[15] did attend government schools was not mentioned. Also overlooked were some of the most important reasons why there were so many in Chinese schools. Government schools were overcrowded, and Chinese had often met with resistance or obstruction when trying to have their children admitted to them. Furthermore, many of the Chinese schools were able to maintain higher standards than government schools, because of greater financial resources for salaries, equipment, buildings and so on.

There were a certain number of nationalist-minded Peranakans who wanted their children to have a purely Chinese education. Another group, perhaps equally large, wanted only to give their children the best education they could afford, regardless of whether the orientation was Chinese, Dutch, religious, or Indonesian nationalist. The majority, however, would probably have preferred an education in which language and curriculum were adjusted to life in Indonesia, but which also included courses giving a general knowledge of China's cultural heritage, including language, literature, history, and philosophy.

In a public statement concerning Takdir Alisjahbana's motion, BAPERKI defended the constitutional rights of citizens to a free choice of education, and of minority groups to the perpetuation of their own cultures.[16]

In May, 1955, BAPERKI held a special conference to discuss education and culture. In a public statement embodying its decisions, the conference

---

15 M. Hutasoit, *Compulsory Education in Indonesia*, (a UNESCO publication printed in the Netherlands), 1954, p. 81.
16 *Berita BAPERKI*, Vol. I, No. 4, July 26, 1954, pp. 2-3.

urged the Government to speed up the expansion and improvement of the public school system, to increase its efforts to prevent discriminatory practices in the schools, to eliminate prejudicial materials from textbooks and teaching materials, and to offer Chinese and other Asian languages in public schools. The conference further proposed that until such time as the schools could meet the educational needs of the whole population, the Government should give as much aid as possible to private schools, and should reject all proposals to exclude citizens from foreign schools. The conference went on record against all schools conducted exclusively for specific groups, including both foreign Chinese Schools and the Government's experimental schools for Chinese. Finally, it was decided that BAPERKI itself should establish, or co-operate in establishing, private Indonesian-language schools open to all, and should gather funds for teacher-training, advanced scholarships, and city dormitories for students from towns where no secondary schooling was available.[17]

During 1956 and 1957, BAPERKI branches did establish a few mixed schools with a "national" curriculum. Newspapers reported the opening of BAPERKI schools, for instance, in Tjilamaja, Kediri, Tanggerang, Bagan Siapi-api, and Kudus. Through Chinese-Indonesian co-operation, similar schools were set up in Jogja and Tandjung Priok. Like the government experimental schools, however, the numbers of mixed schools which were organized privately were too few to offer a satisfactory solution to the problem of Chinese education. During this period, the Ministry of Education was proceeding with discussions and investigations directed towards a policy of providing a national education for all citizen Chinese.

In the summer of 1957, before a national policy had been established, the military commanders of East Indonesia and Central Java took decisive action. In Bali, Lombok, Sumbawa, and Celebes, all foreign Chinese schools were closed. Of the forty-seven schools involved, seven were eventually permitted to reopen, but for foreign students only. Citizen Chinese children were transferred into state schools and newly established private schools with a national curriculum. In Makassar the Government opened a new experimental school, but most of the one thousand citizen Chinese pupils who had been studying in foreign schools were distributed among

---

17 *Kuangpo*, Semarang, June 1, 1955.

fifty different national schools. The commander of the armed forces in Central Java took similar action.

The policy of the military commanders was quickly adopted by the Ministry of Education. In one area after another, foreign schools were closed and citizen Chinese children were redistributed to national schools. In many cities and towns special committees were set up to assist in providing for the ousted pupils. BAPERKI and other Chinese organizations took an active part in the process. Many of the closed foreign schools were converted to state or private "national" schools - for instance, fifteen in Medan and twenty in Djakarta. Some of the larger foreign schools were split in half, with one section for foreign pupils and one for citizens. Many Peranakan children were transferred to regular state schools, but the majority remained segregated not only from alien Chinese but also from Indonesian children. The Ministry of Education permitted Chinese to be taught as a foreign language in the unsubsidized schools, and even allowed them to retain foreign teachers. But by the end of 1957, virtually all citizen Chinese children were in schools teaching the national curriculum in the Indonesian language.

These changes caused disruption and consternation in the Chinese community. There was considerable dissatisfaction and complaint about the "method" the Government employed to achieve its end. But neither the Chinese press nor the public spokesmen of the Chinese community questioned the goal: the elimination of foreign-language, foreign-content education for citizens of Indonesia.

Economic Measures Concerning Citizens of Chinese Descent

As we have seen, under Iskaq Tjokrohadisurjo the Ministry of Economic Affairs undertook a vigorous policy intended to reduce the importance of Chinese in the economy of Indonesia. The program was not confined to restrictions upon foreign Chinese. Citizens of Chinese descent were also subject to considerable limitation in their economic opportunities.

The Governments position on this matter was that a program intended to build up an Indonesian entrepreneurial class could not be called discriminatory. The aim was to create a "harmonious" middle class in which Chinese and Indonesians would co-operate on an equal basis and for the common welfare. In the past, Indonesians had not taken their rightful place in business enterprise because of tradition and because of restrictions placed upon them by the colonial regime. As a result the economy had come to be controlled entirely by non-Indonesians, and the Indonesians themselves were known as a "nation of coolies and a coolie among nations." Under such circumstances, it was only fitting that the Government should do everything in its power to enable Indonesians to acquire the qualities and attributes (including capital) of entrepreneurs.[18]

The Ministry of Economic Affairs, therefore, proposed that Chinese entrepreneurs, of whatever citizenship, should find Indonesian business partners, and make them co-directors and joint-owners of their firms. The statutes of such firms should guarantee that at least fifty per cent of the company's shares should be owned by native Indonesians. In most cases, however, the Indonesian partner would not have sufficient initial capital, and therefore should be given one half of the company's shares at the outset, with the understanding that he would gradually pay for them out of his share of the profits. Furthermore, existing Chinese firms should reorganize their management staff in such a way as to allow the participation of native Indonesians, and Chinese-owned factories should offer facilities for training Indonesian technicians. In these ways the Chinese business community was called upon to aid the Government's program of creating a middle class in which Indonesians would play their just part.

The program was to be voluntary, but in practice the Government had considerable power to enforce it. Iskaq, the Minister of Economic Affairs, announced that foreign credits were to be divided as follows: 15% to foreign concerns, 15% to "non-indigenous" Indonesian concerns (that is, Peranakan concerns), and 70% to "national" concerns. The privileged category of "national" concerns included firms in which up to 50% of the capital was owned by foreigners or citizens of foreign descent. In connection with every economic opportunity which the Ministry of Economic Affairs made available to private businesses - credit facilities, import licenses, wholesale rights, foreign exchange, and so on - -applicants were required to give information on the ownership of their firms, and priorities were given to those in which native Indonesian capital played the largest part.

---

18 *Times of Indonesia*, July 19, 1954.

As in the case of foreign-Chinese businessmen, citizens of Chinese descent found their enterprises hard hit by the new program, and they reacted in the same variety of ways. Some found new outlets for their capital in fields not dependent on imports and foreign exchange. Others put their capital largely into non-productive savings, in the hope that a change of Government would bring better times. And a certain number resorted to bribery or the illegal buying of licenses from Indonesian "front" enterprises. However, a fairly large number did establish new firms jointly-owned with Indonesian partners.

Beyond encouraging the joint-ownership of new and existing firms, the Ministry of Economic Affairs stimulated and aided the establishment of independent native-Indonesian enterprises. In May, 1954, Iskaq issued a circular urging local authorities to canalize industries into the hands of native Indonesian entrepreneurs. In some cases this was done at the expense of the Chinese. For instance, in West Borneo, where coconut-oil factories were entirely in the hands of foreign and foreign-descent Chinese, one-half of these enterprises were turned over to native Indonesian entrepreneurs, and the Head of the provincial Department of Industry stated that the production of rubber, soap, and other commodities would also be transferred in due time.[19]

In June, 1954, the Government issued Regulation PP42, concerning the control of rice mills. According to Article 10 of this decree, "persons having a citizenship other than Indonesian citizenship" were prohibited from ownership, part-ownership, or even shareholding in rice-milling enterprises. Such persons were required to sell or rent their entire rice-mill interests to native Indonesian entrepreneurs within a period of nine months.

In Java, the main rice-producing island of Indonesia, there were 508 rice-mills in 1954. About 400 of these were owned by citizens of Chinese descent, and the rest divided among foreigners and native Indonesian owners. The question arose as to whether the prohibition of ownership was intended to apply only to foreigners, or also to Chinese-descent citizens of Indonesia. Technically, since the latter were still also Chinese citizens under Chinese law, they did "have a citizenship other than Indonesian.. If the regulation were not intended to apply to them, the simple word "foreign" would have been used instead of the complicated

---

19 *Times of Indonesia*, July 19, 1954.

and ambiguous longer phrase. It seemed certain that the Government intended to eliminate all persons of Chinese descent from this field of economic activity.

The regulation aroused vigorous criticism from the Chinese press, and BAPERKI mobilized a campaign against it. The Catholic Party issued a public statement strongly condemning the regulation as a form of discrimination, and politicians of other parties expressed their disapproval. Either because the Government was impressed by the extent of the opposition, or because the plan proved to be impracticable, Iskaq finally announced in September that the prohibition was not intended to apply to Chinese-descent citizens, but only to foreigners.

In early 1956, the Government announced a new policy affecting Peranakan firms. In order to qualify for the privileges reserved for "national" importers, all of the owners of an enterprise would have to be Indonesian citizens whose parents were born in Indonesia. This superceded Iskaq's requirement that 50% of the capital of a "national" firm must be owned by "indigenous" Indonesians. The Chinese press welcomed the elimination of racial discrimination in this respect, but pointed out that very few Chinese were in a position to prove the birthplace of their parents.

Under the second Ali Sastroamidjojo cabinet, the same definition of "national" enterprises was applied, but among the national firms, those owned by "indigenous" Indonesians were given preference. Minister of Trade Sunardjo of the Djuanda cabinet extended this policy. In a public statement, he referred to "indigenous" businessmen as the "favorite child" of the Government.[20]

A large number of Chinese have gradually come to believe that, in spite of its protestations to the contrary, the Government intends to discriminate against them whether they are Indonesian citizens or not. In addition to the policies outlined above, one other important law leads them to this conviction. The Dutch law of 1875 which prohibits the alienation of native-owned land to persons of foreign descent has been perpetuated by the Indonesian Government. This means that with few exceptions Indonesian citizens of Chinese descent cannot buy farm land today. Most Chinese do not care to buy such land, and many admit that

---

20 *Republik*, September 25, 1957.

without the law a highly undesirable problem of Chinese landlordism might arise. Nevertheless, they consider the law to be a touchstone of Government attitude. If the Government were really non-discriminatory, they say, it would protect the farmer from the danger of losing his land to native Indonesian landlords as well as to Chinese.

In reply to this objection, Government authorities maintain that it takes a long time to change a whole system of laws, especially where there is a shortage of legal experts and a large number of urgent legal and legislative problems, as in Indonesia. Therefore, they say, discriminatory laws inherited from Dutch times should not be blamed on the present Government; and as for the measures initiated by the Government, their purpose is not to discriminate, but to bring about a more just distribution of wealth and income among all groups of the population.

Political Parties and the Minority Question

From about 1953 to 1957 or 1958, the Government's minority policy and its attitude on various minority issues were primarily a reflection of the position of the major Government party during this period, the Nationalist Party (PNI). Although the Government-supporting parties had much the same outlook, they did not join the PNI in taking public responsibility for Government minority policy. Spokesmen for the PNI, including Iskaq and other Government officials of that party, publicly explained and defended the economic regulations, the citizenship certificates, and other measures unpopular with the Chinese. It is probable that their arguments and attitudes obtained considerably approval, even among Government opponents who were publicly more favorable to the Chinese minority.

The Indonesian Communist Party (PKI), although generally supporting the PNI-led cabinet, occasionally expressed its disagreement on minorities policy. In the view of the PKI, Indonesian citizens of Chinese descent were to be considered a national force necessary to Indonesia in its struggle against imperialist capital. Therefore, there was no reason to try to substitute native Indonesians for citizens of Chinese descent in various positions; but, on the contrary, the Government should also protect the latter against the competition of the big European companies.[21]

---

21 This is the position stated by PKI leader Sudjito at a mass rally in Surabaja on July 4, 1954, as reported in *Keng Po*, Djakarta, July 6, 1954.

In August, 1954, the central council of the Catholic Party issued a public appeal for the recognition of equal rights for all citizens regardless of religion, race, or locality. Among its specific recommendations were the following: The state should not discriminate between native and foreign-descent citizens in economic matters, such as the allocation of licenses, recognition of import firms, industrial development, and so on. All schools must be open to any Indonesian citizen without exception. Appointments to any type of position should be based solely upon ability, and not upon native origin. The discriminatory colonial agrarian law should be abrograted.[22]

Although explicitly interested primarily in the welfare of the Arab minority, the modernist Islamic party, the Masjumi, issued a statement in April, 1955, calling for the immediate elimination of all discriminatory government measures such as travel permits and citizenship certificates. It also urged its members to do everything in their power to avert anything which might be considered discriminatory in social life and interrelationships between groups.[23]

The Socialist Party (PSI) opposed the minorities policy of the Government on the grounds that it was a violation of the principle of absolute equality of rights for all citizens. The Government's economic measures, they said, had created a class of economic parasites instead of a "national middle class." Worse yet, the Government's efforts had only made the minority problem more difficult. One Socialist writer described the situation as follows:

Indonesians, who were treated as a minority by the Dutch dominant group before the revolution, have now become the dominant group themselves. And this new dominant group, which holds political power, wants to use its political position to achieve a pre-eminent position in social and economic fields as well.

Thus the Government is stimulated to carry out discrimination against groups of citizens who are not considered to be pure Indonesians. The weaker the Government, the greater is its tendency

---

22 *Sin Min*, Semarang, August 24, 1954.
23 *Kuangpo*, Semarang, April 15, 1955.

to yield to popular prejudice, and especially when, in reality, such sentiments find approval in the Government's own inner feelings. As a result, devious methods and legal artifices are found by which to carry out discriminatory practices against the minority, which increasingly feels itself to be treated unjustly.

The reaction on the side of the minority will certainly be to unite itself in minority-type organizations, to increase mutual co-operation, land to struggle against discrimination. This reaction will raise further prejudice on the side of the majority, and will be considered as grounds for increasing discrimination. Thus occurs a reciprocal division and discord which has no end and which greatly worsens the situation.[24]

Thus the opposition parties were able to point out many injustices and undesirable results arising from the Government's minorities policy. How different the general policy might have been under a cabinet comprised of the opposition parties, however, is open to question. The certificates of citizenship condemned by the Masjumi were originally initiated in a Home Affairs Ministry headed by a prominent member of the Masjumi. Under a Socialist Minister, the Economic Affairs Ministry had also planned measures to give special aid to the disadvantaged native Indonesian group. And the proposal to prohibit citizens of foreign descent from attending foreign schools, which was originated by a member of the PSI, did more to alienate the Chinese minority than the Government's educational policies had done.

Two events in 1956 brought the Chinese minority question more directly into the political field: the "Han-Harjono affair" and the "Assaat Movement." The first of these, which originated in a street fight between a Chinese and an Indonesian army officer, rapidly became a national issue. Feelings of hostility and outrage were directed not only against Han, who was accused of trying to use bribes in the legal proceedings which followed the incident, but against all Chinese. Threatening leaflets were distributed and posted throughout the predominantly Chinese quarters of several cities. Strongly anti-Chinese statements were made in

---

24 S. K., "Tentang Kewarganegaraan," *Sikap*, Vol. VII, No. 41, November 1, 1954, p. 2.

public and reported in the press. Several incidents of violence occurred, including the bombing of a Chinese store. Commenting on the reasons why so many Indonesians seemed to approve of such action, an army officer said in a public statement:

> The explosion of the bomb in a car store, which constituted an extra-legal act by the people, did not raise any feeling of regret or horror, but instead it raised laughter and scorn. All of this was because the destruction of the store did not cause any disruption or injury to their own interests, because the group which owned the store is very far from their lives and from the world of their thoughts.[25]

This officer went on to say that the distance between the two groups was due to inequality, with "extraordinary poverty, sorrow, and suffering" on one side, and "wealth and happiness unlimited" on the other. The one side, he asserted, may be said to live off the garbage thrown away by the other.[26]

The Han-Harjono affair brought anti-Chinese feeling to its highest point since Indonesian independence. It not only encouraged people to speak out against the Chinese, but undoubtedly also contributed to the influence of Assaat, a veteran politician, who was leading a campaign for increased economic discrimination against the Chinese. It was only a few months after the Han-Harjono incident that Assaat and his supporters convinced the All-Indonesian National Economic Congress (KENSI) to adopt a resolution urging that all foreign and "non-indigenous" enterprises be transferred as soon as possible to "indigenous" businessmen.[27] Many other Indonesian organizations, especially those concerned with business and trade, went on record in support of Assaat. In some places, "Assaat Associations" were formed.

Among the political parties, the Masjumi was most affected by the Assaat movement. It moved away from its anti-discrimination stand of 1955, and called for aiding the "economically weak" against the "economically strong.. The Masjumi Congress of December 1956 urged

---

25 *Indonesia Raja*, July 12, 1956.
26 *Ibid.*
27 *Times of Indonesia*, August 14, 1956.

that citizens of Arab descent be considered "indigenous," thus exempting them from the discrimination proposed for other foreign-descent citizens - that is, for the Chinese.[28] Two Masjumi representatives in Parliament (though not speaking for the party) attacked the Chinese as having no morals in economic matters and as being "oppressors, extortionists, and smugglers" who were impeding national development.[29]

The Socialist Party (PSI) was also influenced by the Assaat Movement. It issued a confidential statement on the matter, intended for members only. The document leaked to the left-wing press, however, and became a public issue. The full text was finally printed in the Peranakan paper *Keng Po*. Although the statement supported the anti-discriminatory stand which the PSI had taken, it took an equivocal position with regard to the Assaat Movement. Describing the movement as "understandable" and "natural," it stated that it would constitute "no problem" if PSI members participated in the Assaat Movement "when they felt that circumstances called for it.. In closing, it said, "In general we as socialists defend and side with groups which are economically weak."[30]

The PSI's private position, as revealed in this document, reflected an ambivalence in attitudes and a divergence of member alignments which undoubtedly existed in other parties as well. The 1956 PNI Congress in Semarang publicly opposed discrimination[31]; yet that party had been responsible for many discriminatory measures when it was in power. Other parties which took public stands against the policies which were being advocated by Assaat were: the Nahdlatul Ulama (the major Islamic rival of the Masjumi), the Catholic Party, the Communist Party (PKI), and the Murba Party (leftist).[32] In addition, several national organizations and a number of prominent leaders - Islamic, Christian, socialist, and communist - publicly opposed Assaat policies.[33]

Thus Assaat failed to win sufficient political support to change government policy. During 1957 his movement waned, and in 1958 his leadership of pro-discrimination forces came to an end when he defected to the Sumatra rebels. The influence of the Masjumi party, which was

28 *Ibid.*, January 3, 1957.
29 *Suluh Indonesia*, November 13, 1957; and *Republik*, November 22, 1957.
30 *Keng Po*, November 10, 1957.
31 *Berita BAPERKI*, October 15, 1956.
32 *Ibid.*
33 *Ibid.*, and *Republik*, October 23, 1957.

accused of being sympathetic to the rebels, also declined. Subsequent conferences of the All-Indonesian National Economic Congress took a more moderate stand on the issue of economic discrimination.[34]

In summary, it may be said that all major political parties in Indonesia espouse equality and justice for citizen minorities. They agree with government pronouncements that, in order to speed the assimilation process towards a "homogeneous" society, policy should be directed towards winning the loyalty of minorities. On the other hand, all parties favor special measures to assist the economically weak and to limit the strong. Except in the view of the most left-wing parties, which are not interested in developing a native capitalist class, "assisting the economically weak" means privileges for indigenous Indonesians which are not open to citizen Chinese. Furthermore, no party is completely free from historic anti-Chinese prejudices. Thus policy towards minorities, under any Indonesian government, will be a compromise between a desire to avoid racial discrimination and a desire to restrict the Chinese in such a way as to promote long-range economic equality for the majority.

The Possibility of Severe Persecution

The sociologist cannot help but observe that there still exist in Indonesia many of the factors which could provoke outright persecution of the Chinese minority. Economic competition, prejudice, hostility, and considerable segregation provide a situation in which drastic measures or violent actions might be expected. In addition, Indonesia has passed through periods of economic and military crisis in which scapegoats would have been welcome. It is of interest, therefore, to consider the reasons why severe persecution has not occurred (at least not since the end of the revolutionary war), and to reflect on whether it could occur in the future.

Factors which have prevented persecution may be outlined briefly as follows: 1) Acceptance of humanitarian, equalitarian, and scientific ideals makes the display of racial prejudice unacceptable to many Indonesians. 2) There is widespread concern to have Indonesia accepted internationally as a democratic and progressive nation. 3) The most respected national leaders, Soekarno and Hatta, as well as some less well-known leaders,

---

34 Antara, October 13, 1958; PIA, April 10, 1958; and PIA, November 2, 1958.

have consistently opposed racial discrimination. 4) The powerful left-wing parties oppose anti-Chinese action, not only because they are against racism but because they want to maintain friendly relations with Communist China. 5) Many influential political leaders have close ties with Chinese businessmen. 6) Continued opposition to the Dutch has minimized the need for any other scapegoat.

In the opinion of the writer, the number of these factors which are likely to continue to exist will be sufficient to avert drastic persecution in the foreseeable future. If, however, an anti-democratic and anti-Communist regime should ever come to power in Indonesia, drastic measures against the Chinese might be taken or allowed by the government.

CHAPTER EIGHT
INDONESIAN CHINESE ATTITUDES TOWARDS CITIZENSHIP

Government Expectations

In a radio speech to all foreigners during the option period 1949-51, the Head of the Bureau of Minorities Affairs said, in part:

> ...those who intend to choose Indonesian citizenship must wholeheartedly love the country and the people that they are about to choose, because it is love for the country and its people that must be the primary basis and most important element in deciding to choose or to reject in this case. More rational calculations also should not be neglected. But such considerations must not be made basic.[1]

A spokesman of the Nationalist Party (PNI), in a public speech before a Peranakan group, maintained that citizenship cannot mean mere residence in a certain country based upon considerations of personal interest, but must also involve responsibilities, especially the responsibility to do everything possible to serve the interests of the nation.[2]

Chinese Motives in Choosing Indonesian Citizenship in the 1949-51 Option Period

While Indonesian nationalists would like to have Chinese choose Indonesian citizenship only for idealistic reasons, we must assume that in the great majority of the 1949-51 options the motives were otherwise.

---

1 Soewahjo Soemodilogo, "Soal-Soal disekitar Kewarganegaraan," *Siaran Kilat*, No. 22, issued by the Ministry of Information, Djakarta, c. 1951, p. 5.
2 *Suara Merdeka*, Semarang, September 27, 1954.

Divisions and prejudices dating from Dutch times, and fears arising out of the tragedies of revolutionary times left few Chinese with reason to be enthusiastic about the new Indonesia.

Nevertheless, almost all Peranakans regarded Indonesia as their home. Most of them had spent their entire lives there, and had naturally come to love their surroundings as well as their way of life there. For sentimental reasons, many would have liked to "see" China again, or even to die there. But very few had any desire to go back to China to live. They knew that the people and their ways there would be unfamiliar to them. The majority had no desire to live under a Communist government. Furthermore, returning to China was out of the question for most of them because they could not speak Chinese. So the choice before Peranakans was whether to be a citizen or a foreigner in Indonesia.

There was reason to believe that citizenship would involve better relations with the Indonesian Government and people, and better assurances of legal rights and safeguards than could be expected under foreign status. Stringent measures had already been introduced against foreign businesses. But although general discrimination still existed in many cases, such as land ownership, the announced Government policy towards foreign-descent citizens was favorable. And the Provisional Constitution included clear guarantees of equality and freedom for minorities. On the other hand, the Embassy of the People's Republic of China, which was established in Djakarta more than a year before the end of the option period, showed signs of being more interested in winning the goodwill of the Indonesian Government and the people in general than in defending the commercial and legal rights of special groups of Indonesian Chinese.

Finally, although it was not often mentioned publicly, a good many Peranakans no doubt realized that even in accepting Indonesian citizenship they would not be forfeiting Chinese citizenship. If conditions should demand drastic action, therefore, they might hope to obtain the intervention and protection of the Chinese government.

Thus the situation during the option period was such that the self-interests of the Peranakan community, though not entirely clear, appeared to lie in accepting Indonesian citizenship. In the case of those who chose Chinese citizenship, emotional attachments must have outweighed personal interest, except among a small number who intended ultimately to return to China. However, the fact that self-interest was the major motive in choosing Indonesian citizenship should not be considered a condemnation of the Chinese. The history of their position in Indonesia, as we have seen, had given them little reason to be enthusiastic citizens. And it must be remembered that, in spite of this, there was a small but significant number of Chinese who wholeheartedly identified themselves with the revolutionary cause and with the new nation.

Those who passively chose Indonesian citizenship in the 1949-51 option period must now make an active choice under the terms of the Dual Citizenship Treaty with China. This time the penalties for choosing Chinese citizenship are greater, but the future of Indonesian citizens of Chinese descent is still very uncertain. Therefore we may expect options to be made with the same range of motives - mostly practical considerations - as before.

The Question of Good Citizenship

Chinese who have chosen to become Indonesian citizens have many of the attributes of good citizenship as well as certain shortcomings. As mentioned above, they are emotionally tied to the country and to their way of life there. They often express the feeling that, for better or for worse, their destiny lies with Indonesia. Thug they already have one of the indispensable ingredients of patriotism.

The Chinese community in Indonesia has a generally good record for law-abidingness. Its delinquency and crime rates are low, and the community is usually self-disciplined and orderly. On the other hand, in the unusual economic conditions of the past few years, there has been among Chinese an alarming amount of violation or evasion of Government financial and economic regulations. While the proportion of those who are willing to use dishonest methods is probably about the same among other businessmen in Indonesia today, the Chinese are under the heaviest economic restrictions, and are therefore more frequently guilty of business irregularities.

The Chinese have always shown a good deal of public spirit. They have responded quite generously to appeals for contributions to various government and nationalist projects, such as the building of national monuments, municipal stadiums, and so on. Their clinics and hospitals serve a large number of Indonesians as well as Chinese. Their contributions to the relief of victims of floods and volcanic eruptions, and to other charitable causes outside the Chinese community have always been substantial. While it is true that such contributions are motivated partly by the desire to assuage prejudice against them as a minority, they also represent an extension of the traditional Chinese feelings of communal responsibility for those in distress.

The Provisional Constitution stated that every citizen had the right and duty to take part in national defense. Military life is traditionally abhorrent to the Chinese. In 1912, in spite of great community enthusiasm over the recent establishment of a Republican Government in China, the Indies Chinese turned a cold shoulder to the request of the new Government for recruits for its navy.[3] A few years later, when it appeared that the Netherlands Indies might have to defend itself in World War I, a civil defense movement obtained virtually no support from the Chinese.[4] The obligation to fulfill military service if required was one of the conditions of individual assimilation to European legal status which made such assimilation unpopular among the Chinese.

During the war against Japan and the revolutionary war against the Dutch, a certain number of Chinese did serve with the Indonesian forces. In more recent years, BAPERKI has promoted the idea that citizen Chinese should be willing to give military service and that the Armed Forces should be willing to recruit them[5] BAPERKI's youth organization has called upon its members to join in the struggle to regain West New Guinea from the Dutch "by whatever means possible."[6] Thus there appears to be at least a minority of Chinese who would fight for Indonesia if called upon. Many others, perhaps most, would not serve unless conscripted. This does not constitute a problem, however, so long as there has been no need and no desire to recruit Chinese for the Armed Forces.

The Question of Loyalty

Among Indonesian nationalists there is a tendency to question whether the Chinese who have adopted Indonesian citizenship are really loyal to Indonesia. On national holidays they see the Red Chinese flag flying

---

3   *Boekoe Peringetan 1907-1937 Tiong Hwa Siang Hwee Semarang*, Semarang, 1937, p. 8.
4   Liem Thian Joe. *Riwajat Semarang*, Semarang, c. 1933, pp. 232f.
5   See, for instance, *Sin Po*, November 20, 1957.
6   *Sin Po*, January 22, 1958.

alongside the Indonesian flag in front of many shops and residences. Chinese newspapers in the Indonesian language carry frequent articles about China, mostly favorable to the new regime. Chinese schools seem to have pictures of Mao Tse-tung or Sun Yat-sen hanging on every wall. Bookstores are full of translations from Chinese literature, books about China, and comic-books depicting the exploits of Chinese heroes. On the national holidays of the Peking and Taiwan regimes, October 1 and 10 respectively, there used to be rival celebrations in the Chinese community, with decorations, flags, meetings, speeches, and sports events. As we have seen, Kuomintang celebrations have been banned in recent years.

Chinese eager to defend the loyalty of Peranakans claim that these manifestations of Chinese nationalism arise almost entirely from the foreign Chinese community, that the Indonesian-language Chinese papers carry very little more news about China than many non-Chinese papers, and that an interest in Chinese culture indicates nothing about loyalty.

The truth about the orientation of the Indonesian Chinese lies somewhere between these two views. Loyalties are, of course, extremely difficult to assess, and the present writer is well aware that his own conclusions are highly speculative and impressionistic. However, rather than omitting them altogether, or stating them in such general terms as to avoid all possibility of error, the writer will give them in as concrete form as possible, in the hope that they will help the interested reader to come to his own conclusions by comparisons with the statements of other observers.

In trying to get a realistic view of this problem, it will be helpful to distinguish between various kinds of nationalism, and to try to estimate to what extent different groups are characterized by each. For the purposes of this analysis, the present writer will make his own definitions of what appear to him to be three different types of loyalty or nationalism. These three types are not mutually exclusive, and may be combined in the outlook of one person. However, each may also be found alone; therefore separate definitions are justified.

1) *Political Nationalism* is the self-identification of an individual with a nation state. The individual supports the government system of the state, adopts its official ideology, and tends to be willing to sacrifice personal interests to national ones.

2) *Cultural Nationalism* is the self-identification of an individual with the cultural tradition of a nation or people. The individual generally tries to perpetuate the language, literature, philosophy, religion, customs, and habits which he believes to be characteristic of his people. Although he may respect other cultures, he has a strong preference for his own. Political changes within the area of the national culture may be of no concern to him.

3) *Racial Nationalism* is the self-identification of an individual with what he believes to be a certain racial group. The individual is keenly aware of his membership in this racial group, and ascribes to it certain characteristics, mostly favorable. Although he may respect other races, he prefers his own. He tends to restrict his social relations to it, and to disapprove of intermarriages with persons outside it. Political and cultural changes within his racial group may be of no concern to him.

The Chinese nationalist movement which we have described in previous chapters created many political nationalists among the Indies-born Chinese. Perhaps as many as half of all Peranakans considered the Nationalist Government of China as their government during the thirites and forties. And no doubt the majority of Peranakan young people who went to Chinese schools at least passively accepted the ideology of Sun Yat-sen's *San Min Chu I*, or Three Principles of the People. The civil war in China and the establishment of the rival regimes in Peking and Taiwan, however, divided and partly dispelled political nationalism in the Peranakan group. A small and diminishing number remained loyal to the Kuomintang Government. Probably a great number, disapproving of Communism and disillusioned with the Kuomintang, gave up political nationalism. Although these were likely to remain cultural nationalists, this was no bar to their developing political loyalty to Indonesia.

Perhaps the largest sector of the former political nationalists - say, one-quarter of the total Peranakan population - transferred their loyalty to the People's Republic of China. Since the greater part of the 1949-51 option period was after Indonesia's recognition of the Peking Government, it may be assumed that virtually all of the Chinese who rejected Indonesian citizenship belonged to this group. However, not all of the pro-Peking Peranakans rejected Indonesian citizenship.

The extent of political nationalism in the Chinese community is often over-estimated because it is confused with cultural and racial nationalism, which are still very widely prevalent. Racial nationalism can produce pride where it does not produce allegiance; thus there are a great many Indonesian Chinese who take pride in the social, economic, and military achievements of the Chinese people under the new regime. And cultural nationalism can produce interest where it does not produce political loyalty; therefore the classical and modern books, magazines, and art reproductions coming out of Communist China are quite popular among the Indonesian Chinese. Yet the majority of racial and cultural nationalists would not feel any obligation to follow any instructions the Chinese Government might give to its citizens abroad, nor would they be willing to contribute money to any project of that Government. As businessmen and traders, they are not at all attracted to the ideology of Communism, and many of them are strongly opposed to it.

Let us now look at the national orientation of various groups among the Indonesian Chinese, beginning with what we shall call the "passivists." This group, comprising the majority of the Chinese community, is largely made up of shopkeepers, petty traders, and employees of various factories and businesses. Most of these people are apolitical: they believe that it is not wise to get "mixed up" in politics. They intend to be law-abiding Indonesian citizens, but they have no particular feelings of loyalty either to the Indonesian or to the Chinese Government. Cultural nationalism, though common among them, is diminishing slowly. Most of them can speak no more than a few words of Chinese. Western and modernist influences are modifying their family system, and ancestor worship is dying out. Racial nationalism, however, is still relatively strong in this group.

A much smaller, yet significant, group of "passivists" is made up of disillusioned intellectuals. The idealism and modern ideas of these people had to some extent broken down their racial nationalism, while their Western educations had made inroads on their cultural nationalism. Originally they identified themselves with the revolution, or at least placed high hopes in the future of the Indonesian Republic. But the hard realities of the post-revolutionary period have disappointed them, especially the fact that they have not been treated with full equality. Since their Western outlook precludes loyalty to Communist China, they have no strong national allegiance.

We come now to the "participationists." This group includes the majority of the formal and informal leaders of the Indonesian Chinese community, most newspaper editors and correspondents, a large section of the more well-to-do businessmen, and a representation from other groups as well. Motivated to some extent by broad idealism, but more often mainly by minority group interests, these people have decided to participate actively in Indonesian politics and citizenship. There are a few among them who are politically loyal primarily to the Peking Government, and to the Indonesian Government only in so far as the two loyalties do not conflict. The majority, however, are non-Communist or anti-Communist, and give no allegiance to China. President Soekarno's *Pantjasila*, the official ideology of the Indonesian state, is congenial to their way of thinking, and they favor parliamentary democracy. On the other hand, their feelings towards any particular Administration tend to depend largely upon its policy towards the Chinese. There is a good deal of racial and cultural nationalism among them.

Finally, there are the "assimilationists." This is perhaps the smallest group. Assimilationists are found at all levels of the Chinese community, but chiefly among those who have attended Dutch- or Indonesian-language schools. The fundamental belief of this group is that the Chinese community must endeavor to merge itself into the society and culture of the majority of Indonesian citizens as rapidly as possible. Some assimilationists are would-be Chinese racial or cultural nationalists who believe that the only way for Chinese to survive in the new society is to give up their "Chineseness." Others are those who have already identified whole-heartedly with the Indonesian people and have no Chinese nationalist tendencies. Both agree that the "participationists," by defending the rights and perpetuating the distinctness of their own group, only increase the prejudices of the majority and make the minority problem even more difficult to solve. The assimilationists believe that instead of trying to improve their position through their own organizations, Chinese-descent citizens should join and work through the political parties of the majority. Many are already doing so.

Passivists, participationists, and assimilationists are loyal in the sense that they all recognize the authority of the Indonesian Government and of none other. Among the last two groups, there is a minority who are loyal also in the sense of positive feelings of attachment, affinity, and responsibility. At the other extreme there is a fourth group who give allegiance to the Peking or the Taiwan Government. Most of these are alien Chinese. A large proportion of alien Chinese, however, are either apolitical or deliberately neutral.

The majority of Chinese schools, at least until 1957, promoted loyalty to one Chinese government or the other, with flags, emblems, pictures, songs, and textbooks attuned to this purpose. It is estimated that in the four years 1951-54, some 12,000 students left Indonesia for China, with no expectation of ever returning. Most Totok associations, including those supposedly based only on local or provincial place of origin in China, gave their allegiance to either Mao Tse-tung or Chiang Kai-shek. The majority of Peranakan associations attempted to remain neutral, but they were often identified as being pro-Peking or pro-Taiwan depending upon which side had won most of the leading positions.

As we have seen, openly pro-Kuomintang schools and organizations were suppressed and disbanded during the Sumatra revolt. Communist China, on the other hand, has continued to win the loyalty of new "converts" every year, primarily among young people. This is probably due as much to pressures within Indonesia as to attraction from China itself. The pro-Peking group, however, is more or less regularly depleted by "return" emigration to China.

Trends in Chinese Orientations to Minority Group Problems

Let us now consider the recent history of Chinese minority group organization. When the Persatuan Tionghoa was formed in 1948, its whole emphasis was on defending the position of the Chinese minority. Although the membership was almost entirely Peranakan, they believed in the necessity of unity within the entire Chinese community, and defended the right of Totoks to treatment as favorable as that given to the subjects of any other foreign country. Their defense of the right of minorities to preserve their own language and culture and to maintain their own schools was an indication of strong cultural nationalism.

Not long afterwards, the Persatuan Tionghoa was reorganized as a political party, the "Partai Democrat Tionghoa Indonesia," or the Democratic Party of Indonesian Chinese. Its major mission was to achieve equal rights for Indonesian citizens of Chinese descent and to oppose discrimination. Thus it was wholly what we have called "participationist."

But this party received little support from the Chinese community, and was able to establish only about twenty branches in six years. The main reason for this was the traditional political apathy of the Chinese. But there was a growing feeling among Chinese leaders that the minority group could not improve its position through an organization which was exclusively Chinese and which worked solely for the interests of the minority.

As a result, a conference of representatives from the Partai Democrat Tionghoa Indonesia and several other Chinese minority organizations met in Djakarta in March, 1954, to establish a new political organization with broader aims. Thus BAPERKI (Badan Permusjawaratan Kewanganegaraan Indonesia) came into existence, and the previous parties and organizations were officially disbanded. Literally translated, BAPERKI'S full name means "Consultative Body on Indonesian Citizenship." This name was intended to indicate that it was not just another political parity, nor an exclusively Chinese organization. In terms of our analysis, it was an attempt to unite participationists and assimilationists in one organization.

BAPERKI was still participationist in that it was primarily a minority group organization which would struggle against all forms of discrimination and would put up its own candidates for the new Parliament. On the other hand, it represented a certain shift of opinion and practice towards the assimilationists point of view. Membership was opened to persons of all national origins, and a few non-Chinese did participate. The chairman of the Surakarta branch, for instance, was a native Indonesian. Then too, BAPERKI included a number of Chinese assimilationists who were already active members of major political parties, and it supported their candidacy in the national elections. While working for the achievement of the rights of citizenship, the new organization also stressed the fulfillment of the duties of citizenship and the incorporation of the minority group into the general body politic.

BAPERKI's 1955 stand on education was an example of the attempt to combine "participationism" and "assimilationism." On the one hand, it proposed that minority group citizens should be allowed to send their children to foreign schools, at least for an interim period, and that the Chinese language (and other Asian languages) should be offered in the government schools. On the other hand, it opposed all exclusive schools, and proposed to help in building up a national school system in which children of Indonesian and Chinese descent would learn to be good Indonesian citizens in the same classrooms .

In spite of these compromises with "assimilationism," BAPERKI did not go far enough to suit most assimilationists. Even within BAPERKI the issue was far from settled. The large Surabaja branch split over the question of whether the organization should run its own candidates for election. Many considered that the constitutional guarantee of a certain number of parliamentary seats for minority group members tended to perpetuate rather than to alleviate the minority problem. And the 1955 BAPERKI conference on education and culture did not reach any conclusion as to whether a minority group should aim to perpetuate and develop its own culture, or shake it off in favor of the majority culture. There were Chinese cultural nationalists in BAPERKI, as well as assimilationists.

As we have seen, anti-Chinese feeling increased in 1956 and 1957, and the Government instituted several decisive measures, such as the redistribution of citizen Chinese pupils in "national" schools. These events convinced more and more Chinese that rapid voluntary assimilation would be the only way to minimize discrimination. Virtually the entire Peranakan press supported the aims of the new national education policy. Several Chinese newspapers, including the influential *Keng Po*, opposed special minority group representation in Parliament and the Constituent Assembly on the grounds that it would aggravate rather than reduce hostility between groups. And although BAPERKI spokesmen urged the Government to appoint BAPERKI candidates to the minority seats, they declared that they had never asked for guaranteed representation for minority groups.

Trends toward assimilationist thinking and toward an Indonesian rather than a Chinese orientation were also evident in the field of voluntary associations. Increasingly, Chinese spokesmen and editors were advocating the transformation of specifically Chinese organizations operating in the public realm, such as the Chinese Chambers of Commerce, the Chung Hua Tsung Hui federations, and Chinese student associations. They suggested that Indonesian names should be substituted for the Chinese names of these organizations, and that native Indonesians should be encouraged to become members in place of alien Chinese. Accordingly, many commercial, professional, and sports organizations did change their names and open their memberships to non-Chinese. For instance, in 1957 the Chinese university students' Ta Hsűeh Hsűeh Sheng Hui became the Perhimpunan Mahasiswa Indonesia, and the secondary school students' Chung Lien Hui became the Perkumpulan Peladjar Sekolah Menengah Indonesia. Such changes were probably somewhat accelerated by the Army Chief of Staff's proclamation urging citizen Chinese not to mix with alien Chinese but with native Indonesians in their social and organizational life. The habits of segregation are strong, however, and some of the reasons for it still exist. It seems likely, therefore, that the number of genuinely mixed organizations is still rather small.

A further indication that the orientation of many Chinese-descent citizens has been turning away from China may be seen in the growing number of Chinese who have joined Christian churches. In the city of Semarang, for instance, where there were very few Chinese Christians three decades ago, almost 10% of the Chinese population is now either Catholic or Protestant, and the rate of increase considerably accelerated in the post-revolutionary years. For these people, joining a church is a sure indication of the absence of political loyalty to Communist China. Although Chinese Christians may be cultural or racial nationalists, they are not likely to be political nationalists.

While the Catholic church is broadly tolerant of cultural differences, the Protestant church has a stronger tendency to draw its Chinese converts away from cultural nationalism. Chinese Christians may remain "passivists" with regard to Indonesian citizenship, but their churches place a steady pressure upon them to become politically active by supporting the Protestant and Catholic political parties. These two parties are the best examples of Chinese-Indonesian political co-operation to date. On the other hand, while there are many individual assimilationists among Chinese Christians, the policy of the churches has not been assimilationist. Unlike the Catholic Church, the Chinese and Indonesian Protestant Churches are entirely separate. Occasionally even in the Catholic Church the lay organizations are segregated.

Summary

In this survey of the attitudes of the Indonesian Chinese, we have found only a small number who are primarily loyal to either the Peking or the Taiwan Government. There is likewise only a small number who give wholehearted allegiance to the Indonesian Government. Most Chinese are racial and cultural nationalists, but not political nationalists. Between the Indonesian patriots on the one hand and the partisans of Peking and Taiwan on the other, there is a very large group of citizen Chinese who accept the jurisdiction of the Indonesian Government. This group comprises those whom we have called "passivists," "participationists," and "assimilationists ." Because of the sharpening of political issues both internationally and locally, the number of passivists, who have no positive national loyalties, is diminishing. A growing number of Chinese see no alternative but to accept their Indonesian citizenship seriously. Many of these do so with a determination to participate as a separate group in Indonesian society, while opposing discrimination. Others believe that rapid voluntary assimilation is the only way to avoid discrimination or even persecution. In recent years, there has been a trend towards the assimilationist point of view as well as an increase in manifestations of loyalty. But discrimination and public condemnation, as well as traditional segregation and prejudice on both sides, have greatly impeded progress towards assimilation and wholehearted allegiance.

CHAPTER NINE

CONCLUSIONS AND PROSPECTS

Government Policy: Past and Future

Our detailed review of government policy towards the Indonesian Chinese, of the statements of government spokesmen and the measures of government agencies, has shown a somewhat bewildering picture. On the one hand, the Government has appeared dilatory, disingenuous, and discriminatory in its treatment of the Chinese. Heavy pressure has been applied against the alien Chinese. Citizen Chinese have often found themselves treated as aliens or "second-class citizens." With regard to national status, proof of citizenship, and various forms of economic discrimination, the Indonesian Chinese have gone through long periods of uncertainty and frustration. On the other hand, declared policy has always been against racial discrimination. The legal and constitutional rights of the Chinese are comparable to those of minorities in the most progressive countries. The extent to which Chinese have been permitted to take part in politics has been commendable. Short-sighted or discriminatory policies, at both the national and the local levels, have frequently been withdrawn or modified when opposed by the Chinese community.

Before attempting to interpret and assess this dualism in policy, we may note that it has two consequences which are undesirable from the Government's point of view. Firstly, economic discrimination and administrative harassment tend to alienate the citizen Chinese, thus jeopardizing the goals of assimilation and allegiance. Secondly, repeated changes, modification, and rectifications of policy encourage the Chinese not to comply with discriminatory or burdensome regulations when they are first issued; there is a tendency to "wait and see."

In order to interpret this dualism in policy, we shall consider four major factors: government structure, public and official attitudes, the passage of time, and the nature of alternative policies. With regard to structure, it is significant that policy affecting the Chinese has been made by many different government bodies acting separately. The Army, the Legislature, the Bureau of Minority Affairs, the police Department, the Inspectorate of Foreign Education, the Immigration Department, the Alien Control Bureau, and at least four different ministries have promulgated regulations concerning the Chinese. It is apparent that this has usually been done with little mutual consultation and without co-ordination at the cabinet level. As a result, many decisions have been made which later had to be modified or reversed in order to reconcile them with national policy or the policies of other agencies.

A second structural reason for inconsistent policies is that regional, district, and local government bodies have had sufficient autonomy or lack of supervision to allow them to initiate their own policies towards the Chinese. Again and again, official actions at the local level have required modification or rectification at higher levels. The fact that there has been inadequate communication and co-ordination between national government bodies, and between these bodies and local agencies, accounts for much of the dualism in policy. With regard to treatment of the Chinese, then, the Government should not be thought of as a monolithic body which cannot make up its mind. It is an exceedingly complex structure, with many minds.

Turning now to public and official attitudes, it must be recognized that Indonesians, as individuals, are not single-minded in their view of the Chinese. Having felt the stigma of racial inferiority under colonial rule, and having fought a revolution at least partly for democratic and humanitarian ideals, most Indonesians are ideologically opposed to racial discrimination. But as we have seen in Chapter I, the colonial regime bred social exclusivenesss and superiority feelings among the Chinese, and allowed them to take a dominant position in the economy. As a result, the great majority of Indonesians have feelings of dislike, resentment, or hostility toward the Chinese. They cannot regard with indifference the fact that the majority of wealthy people in Indonesia are of Chinese origin.

This dualism in attitudes is sometimes reflected in dualism of policy. It appears that policies are sometimes made primarily on the basis of anti-Chinese feeling, and without sufficient forethought. When the consequences of such policies become apparent, they may be modified in accordance with humanitarian or non-discriminatory principles. The eventual removal of the experimental schools for citizen Chinese from the jurisdiction of the inspectorate of Foreign Education is an example of this kind of reversal. A more striking example is the 1958 discontinuation of the exorbitant fees for court certificates of citizenship.

Apparent inconsistencies in policy are also a result of the fact that, with the passage of time, Governments change and ministers and department heads come and go. Such changes, along with the pressures of urgent problems such as the Sumatra revolt and the abrogation of the Round Table Agreements with Holland, have caused many delays in the solution of problems concerning the Chinese.

In the opinion of the writer, inconsistencies and delays are due also to the fact that the alternative solutions to the "Chinese problem" would both involve certain measures which the Government does not wish to take. One solution which has been proposed is "Indonesianization." This would involve the assimilation of the greatest possible number of Chinese into Indonesian society. Alien Chinese who intend to reside permanently in Indonesia would be encouraged to become citizens, and citizen Chinese would be encouraged to identify themselves with the Indonesian nation and people.

Such a policy would be extremely difficult for any Indonesian Government to put into practice, however, because of the widespread feelings against the Chinese and the desire of most organized groups for economic discrimination against them.

The alternative solution is to maximize the number of alien Chinese, to expel them from the country and to press the citizen Chinese either to emigrate or to give up their favorable position in the economy. This policy, too, would be extremely difficult to put systematically into effect, mainly because Indonesia wants to remain a democratic country in the eyes of the world and to maintain friendly relations with China.

Caught between the problems involved in these alternatives, successive Indonesian Governments have vacillated between them without a commitment to either. As we have seen, announced policy has generally followed the first alternative (accepting and assimilating the Chinese), but actual policy has often been closer to the second (expelling and discriminating against the Chinese).

We have now outlined four major factors which have contributed to dualism in policy towards the Indonesian Chinese. Let us consider future possibilities. With regard to government structure, it may well be that the form of "guided democracy" which is emerging under Soekarno's leadership will make possible better coordination of policy and fewer inconsistencies due to changing personnel at the policy-making level. The tension between ideals and prejudices will doubtless remain, however, as will the obstacles to both alternative policies. It seems likely, therefore, that the dualism in policy will continue. A consistent policy of attraction and assimilation is now virtually impossible not only because of persisting hostility and desires for "economic protection of the weak against the strong," but also because the Dual Citizenship Treaty maximizes the number of Chinese aliens and provides no opportunity for their future naturalization. A consistent policy of discrimination and expulsion would be possible only if an Indonesian Government came to power which was willing to renounce democratic principles and to defy the Government of China.

In the opinion of the writer, it is still possible that a compromise policy could be carried out consistently – one which would gradually minimize the number of alien Chinese by progressively increasing pressure, and which would gradually Indonesianize the citizen Chinese by encouraging assimilation while systematically reducing racial discrimination. In view of the magnitude and number of the problems which the Indonesian Government is facing, however, it seems unlikely that policy toward the Chinese will receive the attention and the vigorous leadership which would be required for success. On the basis of this assumption, let us look at the situation with regard to alien and citizen Chinese separately.

Position of the Foreign Chinese

Until recent years, the foreign Chinese residing in Indonesia held a strong position in the internal economy and predominated in trade with other Asian countries. With their own press, schools, and organizations, they formed a community quite distinct even from the Peranakan community. Although a large proportion of them were apolitical, many were active supporters of either the Peking or the Taiwan Government.

In recent years, government regulations have closed one field of economic activity after another to the alien Chinese. Their schools and newspapers have been severely limited in numbers and are now closely controlled and supervised. They have been heavily taxed. Pro-Kuomintang organizations and activities have been banned.

It appears that, implicitly at least, the policy of the Government has always been to force as many as possible of the alien Chinese to leave the country. This policy was clearly stated by the Minister of Economic Affairs, Iskaq, in 1954:

> We must fight against the capital of foreigners, and we must make every effort to expel them from Indonesia and put Indonesian citizens in their places. If necessary their expulsion must be forced, so that we ourselves can operate their enterprises.[1]

And in November 1957, the Minister of Foreign Affairs, Subandrio, said in Parliament:

> Of course it is the intention of the Government to prepare a law which will fix the maximum number of foreigners who may reside permanently in Indonesia.[2]

In view of the nature of government policy, it seems probable that only a very small number of Indonesia-born Chinese will choose Chinese citizenship in the present option period. We have seen that there is a certain number of citizen Chinese whose real allegiance is to Peking. We have surmised that this number is being augmented by converts who have been attracted to the Communist regime or who have become disillusioned with their status in Indonesia. Probably most such persons will opt for Indonesian citizenship, however, unless they plan to emigrate to China in the very near future. Under the provisions of the treaty, dual nationals who opt for Indonesian citizenship can later regain Chinese citizenship by establishing permanent residence in China.

For these reasons, it is unlikely that the present option period will result in any substantial change in the proportions of citizen and foreign Chinese. There will be close to a million Chinese aliens

---

1   *Suara Merdeka*, September 27, 1954.
2   As reported in Antara, November 22, 1957, and *Sin Po* November 23, 1957.

in Indonesia. The size of this number makes the expulsion policy an extremely difficult one to carry out. Especially for the large number of aliens who have objections against returning to China, expulsion would mean considerable, and sometimes severe, hardship. To this writer it appears unlikely that the present Indonesian Government would risk the disapprobation of world public opinion and the opposition of Communist China which a forced mass expulsion policy would entail. Therefore Indonesia faces the prospect of a large alien Chinese population for many years to come.

Discrimination and pressure will convince many alien Chinese to emigrate. Others will desire naturalization. Even in 1958, many foreign Chinese were requesting naturalization. Many of their descendants, born in Indonesia, will also desire Indonesian citizenship. Since assimilation might be a more feasible solution than expulsion in the case of many aliens and their descendants, it is perhaps unfortunate that naturalization is not possible. But Indonesian law does not allow the naturalization of persons who would not thereby lose their former citizenship, and Chinese law does not revoke the citizenship of persons who acquire a second citizenship. Therefore the naturalization of alien Chinese in Indonesia could only be made possible by a treaty between the two countries. At the time of the 1955 treaty, the policy of the Indonesian Government was to maximize the number of alien Chinese, so there was no reason to ask China for naturalization provisions. It is questionable whether China would have agreed, in any case.

It is now clear that both the mass expulsion and the assimilation solutions to the alien Chinese problem are impossible or extremely unlikely in the near future. The prospect is for a protracted period in which economic pressure and residential restrictions will drive many aliens back to China while many others remain to intensify the problem.

Position of the Citizen Chinese

Indonesian citizens of Chinese descent form a community largely separate from both the native Indonesians and the foreign Chinese. Side by side with the latter, they have held a dominant position in the internal economy of Indonesia. They have exercised their political and legal rights as citizens but have been discriminated against economically and have been subject to a series of administrative harassments (primarily with regard to proving their citizenship) . Their children are no longer permitted to attend Chinese-language schools.

A small proportion of the citizen Chinese are primarily loyal to one or other of the two rival Chinese Governments. The great majority, however, recognize the sole jurisdiction of the Indonesian Government. Many feel little positive loyalty towards Indonesia, but a significant number identify themselves politically with the new nation and intend to carry out the responsibilities and to win the rights of full citizenship. There is also a growing number who believe that complete assimilation into Indonesian society and culture is desirable. Nevertheless, most Peranakans are what we have called "racial and cultural nationalists," though not "political nationalists."

Experience in other parts of the world suggests that racial and cultural group feelings in a minority group are not necessarily incompatible with loyalty to a new nation. Theoretically, the Indonesian Government could win the allegiance of its Chinese-descent citizens without first breaking down their racial and cultural nationalism. Presumably this would be done through a policy of attraction based upon equal treatment for the Chinese minority and a generous attitude towards them. On the other hand, racial discrimination or attacks on their cultural group interests would be expected to reduce the chances of winning their allegiance.

But it is not only allegiance which the Indonesian people want from the Chinese minority. In practice, the Government must take into account other demands as well. As we have seen, native Indonesians want to share in economic well-being on a basis equal with the Chinese. Many demand a leveling process which would allow native Indonesians to take a predominant position in the business class. In addition, they want the Chinese to give up their superiority attitudes, their social exclusiveness, and their distinctive ways. They want total assimilation.

The Government, therefore, has the task of reconciling three aims in its minority policy: allegiance, assimilation, and economic leveling. But measures intended to bring about the latter jeopardize the former two, and attempts to speed assimilation tend to alienate loyalty. As we have seen, commitment to a single consistent policy has been impossible.

It is conceivable that "protection of the economically weak against the strong" could be carried out without racial discrimination, as has been proposed by Soekarno and Hatta. Presumably this would mean assistance to all small businessmen (except aliens), and restrictions on all large-scale businessmen, regardless of racial origin. In addition, it would involve other measures to raise the general standard of living of the people. While such a policy would alienate the wealthiest Chinese (and Indonesians), it would be no obstacle to the assimilation of the rest. But the irrational factors and deep prejudices which have operated in the past still exist. As suggested in the first section of this chapter, dualism in policy is likely to persist for some time to come. Discriminatory measures will continue, as will efforts to conciliate and attract the citizen Chinese. Therefore we can expect only slow progress, with considerable friction and many setbacks, on the road towards the integration of citizen Chinese into Indonesian society.

SUMMARY OF THE MAIN PROVISIONS OF THE INDONESIAN CITIZENSHIP ACT OF 1946 (ACT NO. 3/1946):

1. Citizens of Indonesia are:
   a. Descendants. through both parents, of the original inhabitants of the territory of Indonesia.
   b. Persons not belonging to the group mentioned above, but with one parent who does, who were born and have their residence in Indonesia; and persons not belonging to the group mentioned above, but who were born in the territory of Indonesia and have resided there for the last five years continuously; provided that such per sons do not reject Indonesian citizenship on the grounds of being citizens of another country.
   c. Persons who have gained citizenship through naturalization.
   d. Legitimate, legally-recognized, or adopted children whose parents are Indonesian citizens.
2. A woman's citizenship follows that of her husband as long as she is married. Upon the death of her husband or her divorce from him. She may regain her former citizenship by making an official declaration to the proper authorities.
3. The obtaining or losing of Indonesian citizenship by a man or a widow applies also to his or her unmarried children under twenty-one years of age. However, the children of a woman whose citizenship changes because of a second marriage retain their former citizenship.
4. Persons in category 1. b. above who wish to reject Indonesian citizenship must submit a formal declaration, along with supporting personal documents, to the Justice Department (through their local Court of Justice) within one year after this act comes into effect (April

10. 1946 to April 10. 1947 – but later extended to August 17. 1948).

5. Persons who are at least twenty-one years of age or who are married, and who have resided continuously in Indonesia for five years and are able to speak Indonesian may apply for naturalization. Among the facts that they must be able to document is the following that the laws of their former country constitute no obstacle to this naturalization.

6. When a child who has lost or obtained Indonesian citizenship as a result of the naturalization of his father or mother reaches the age of twenty-one or before that age is married, he may reject his new citizenship within the one year following, and thus retain his former citizenship.

7. Indonesian citizenship is lost:
   a. if the citizenship of another country is obtained, or
   b. if one becomes a soldier or a government employee of another country without the previous consent of the President of Indonesia.

APPENDIX TWO
EXCERPT FROM THE ROUND TABLE AGREEMENT CONCERNING THE ASSIGNMENT OF CITIZENS (NOVEMBER. 1949).[1]

Article 5

Persons who, immediately before the transfer of sovereignty, are of age and are Netherlands subjects of foreign-origin-non-Netherlanders (uitheemse Nederlandse onderdanen-niet-Nederlanders) and who were born in Indonesia or reside in the Republic of the United States of Indonesia shall acquire Indonesian nationality but may, within the time limit therefore stipulated, reject Indonesian nationality.

If, immediately before the transfer of sovereignty, such persons had no other nationality than the Netherlands nationality, they shall regain Netherlands nationality.

If, immediately before the transfer of sovereignty, such persons possessed simultaneously another nationality, they shall, when rejecting Indonesian nationality, regain Netherlands nationality only on the strength of a statement made by them to that effect.

1 United Nations Commission for Indonesia, *Appendices to the Special Report to the Security Council on the Round Table Conference*, United Nations Security Council publication. S/1417/Add. 1. 14 November 1949, p. 84.

APPENDIX THREE
EXCERPT FROM THE PROVISIONAL CONSTITUTION OF THE REPUBLIC OF INDONESIA (ACT NO. 7, GAZETTE NO. 37, AUGUST, 1950):

Article 144

Pending the promulgation of the regulations on citizenship by the law referred to in paragraph 1 of Article 5, all persons who have acquired Indonesian nationality according to or on the basis of the Agreement on the Division of Citizens, attached to the Agreement of Transfer, and those whose nationality has not been determined by said Agreement and who on 27th December. 1949, had acquired Indonesian citizenship according to the law of the Republic of Indonesia prevailing on that date, shall be citizens of the Republic of Indonesia.

EXCERPT FROM THE DRAFT CITIZENSHIP ACT OF 1954[1](UNOFFICIAL TRANSLATION):

Article 4

A foreigner born and having his residence in the territory of the Republic of Indonesia whose father or mother, in accordance with the specifications of Article 1 paragraph a, was also born in the territory of the Republic of Indonesia and at the time of his birth or later resided continuously in the territory of the Republic of Indonesia for a period exceeding ten years, obtains Indonesian citizenship if and when he makes a declaration that he desires Indonesian citizenship and rejects his other citizenship.

This declaration must be made within one year after the person concerned becomes eighteen years of age, at the Court of Justice of his place of residence.

---

1 The full text of the draft act and its accompanying explanations may be found in *Berita BAPERKI*, Djakarta, Vol. I, Nos. 7/8, October-November, 1954, pp. 9-13.

ACT NO. 62 OF THE YEAR 1958 CONCERNING REPUBLIC OF INDONESIA CITIZENSHIP (OFFICIAL TRANSLATION)

Section 1

A Republic of Indonesia citizen shall be:

1. a person who by virtue of laws, agreements and/or regulations operative since the proclamation of Indonesia's independence on August 17, 1945, have become Republic of Indonesia citizens;
2. a person who at birth has legal family relations with his/her father who is a citizen of the Republic of Indonesia, on the understanding that his/her Republic of Indonesia citizenship shall commence at the moment when the afore-mentioned legal family relationship comes into force, and that such relationship shall be entered into before the person concerned has attained eighteen years of age or has married under the age of eighteen;
3. a child born within 300 days after the decease of its father, if the father was a citizen of the Republic of Indonesia at the time of decease;
4. a person whose mother was a citizen of the Republic of Indonesia at the time of his/her birth, if at that time the person concerned had no legal family relationship with his/her father;
5. a person whose mother was a citizen of the Republic of Indonesia at the time of his/her birth, if his/her father has no citizenship or so long as the citizenship of the father is unknown;
6. a person born within the territory of the Republic of Indonesia insofar as the two parents are unknown;
7. a foundling abandoned within the territory of the Republic of Indonesia insofar as the two parents are unknown;

8. a person born within the territory of the Republic of Indonesia in case the two parents are devoid of any citizenship or in case the citizenship of the two parents is unknown;
9. a person born within the territory of the Republic of Indonesia, who at the time of his/her birth did not acquire the citizenship of his/her father or mother, and so long as he/she has not acquired the citizenship of his/her father or mother;
10. a person who has acquired Republic of Indonesia citizenship under the provisions of the present Act.

Section 2

1. An alien child under five years of age who is adopted by a citizen of the Republic of Indonesia shall acquire Republic of Indonesia citizenship if such adoption is validated by the District Court of Justice in the town where the adopting person resides.
2. The validation referred to in the foregoing paragraph shall be applied for by the adopting person within one year after the adoption or within one year after the present Act has come into operation.

Section 3

1. In case a child born out of wedlock from a mother who is a citizen of the Republic of Indonesia, or a child born in wedlock but by a judicial divorce decree given into the custody of the mother who is a citizen of the Republic of Indonesia, follows the citizenship of its father who is an alien. Such child shall be permitted to apply to the Minister of Justice for Republic of Indonesia citizenship, if, upon the acquirement of the Republic of Indonesia citizenship, it has no other citizenship or attaches a statement abjuring the other citizenship in the manner legally provided for by its country of origin and/or in the manner provided for by an agreement for the settlement of dual citizenship between the Republic of Indonesia and the country concerned.
2. The application referred to above shall be made to the Minister of Justice through the intermediary of the District Court or the Representative Office of the Republic of Indonesia in the town where the applicant resides, within one year after the applicant has attained eighteen years of age.

3. With the approval of the Council of Ministers, the Minister of Justice shall allow or refuse such application.
4. Republic of Indonesia citizenship acquired through application shall come into effect on the day when the relative decree of the Minister of Justice is promulgated.

Section 4

1. An alien born and residing within the territory of the Republic of Indonesia, whose father – or mother, in case there is no legal family relationship with the father – was also born in the territory of the Republic of Indonesia and is a resident of the Republic of Indonesia, can apply to the Minister of Justice for acquiring Republic of Indonesia citizenship, if, upon the acquirement of the Republic of Indonesia citizenship, he has no other citizenship or if, at the time of application, he also submits a written statement abjuring any other citizenship he may possess under the legal provisions operative in his country of origin, or under the provisions of an agreement in settlement of dual citizenship entered into between the Republic of Indonesia and the country concerned.
2. The application referred to above shall have been submitted to the Minister of Justice, through the intermediary of the District Court in the town where the applicant resides, within one year after the applicant has attained eighteen years of age.
3. With the approval of the Council of Ministers, the Minister of Justice shall allow or refuse such application.
4. Republic of Indonesia citizenship acquired through such application shall come into effect on the day when the relative decree of the Minister of Justice is promulgated.

Section 5

1. Republic of Indonesia citizenship through naturalization shall have been acquired by the operation of (he Minister of Justice's decree granting such naturalization.
2. To qualify for an application for naturalization,
   a. the applicant must have attained twenty-one years of age;
   b. the applicant must be born within the territory of the Republic of Indonesia or, at the time of application, must have been residing

uninterruptedly in that area for at least the last five years, or, when interrupted, for 10 years in all;

c. the applicant must have the consent of his wife/wives, in case he is a married man;

d. the applicant must be sufficiently proficient in the Indonesian language, have a fair knowledge of Indonesian history, and never have been sentenced for a criminal offence to the prejudice of the Republic of Indonesia;

e. the applicant must be mentally and physically sound;

f. the applicant must pay into the Exchequer an amount varying between Rp. 500 and Rp. 10,000, the definite size of which shall be determined by the Revenue Office in his town of residence, on the basis of his actual monthly income, with the proviso that the aforementioned amount shall not be higher than his actual monthly income;

g. the applicant must have a permanent source of income;

h. the applicant must have no citizenship, or have lost his citizenship upon acquiring Republic of Indonesia citizenship, or attach a statement abjuring his other citizenship under the legal provisions of his country of origin or under the provisions of an agreement in settlement of dual citizenship concluded between the Republic of Indonesia and the country concerned. So long as a woman is married, she shall not be permitted to apply for naturalization.

3. An application for naturalization shall be written on stamped paper, and be submitted to the Minister of Justice through the intermediary of the District Court of the Republic of Indonesia Representative Office in the town where the applicant resides.

The application shall be written in the Indonesian language, and shall be submitted together with documents in evidence of the matters referred to in paragraph (2) excluding item d.

The District Court or the Republic of Indonesia Representative Office concerned shall verify the correctness of the documentary evidence, and test applicant as to his/her proficiency in the use of the Indonesian language and his/her knowledge of Indonesian history.

4. With the approval of the Council of Ministers, the Minister of Justice shall allow or refuse applications for naturalization.

5. The decree of the Minister of Justice granting naturalization, which

becomes effective on the day when the applicant takes the oath, or makes the promise of allegiance before the District Court or the Republic of Indonesia Representative Office in his town of residence shall be retroactive to the day when the afore-mentioned decree is promulgated.

The oath or promise of allegiance shall run as follows:

"I swear (promise) that I abjure all allegiance to any alien authority; that "I recognize and accept the supreme authority of the Republic of Indonesia, "and that I shall remain loyal to it; that I shall uphold and seriously serve the "Constitution and the laws of the Republic of Indonesia; that I shall readily "bear this responsibility without any qualification whatsoever."

6. Upon the applicant having taken the oath, or made the promise, of allegiance referred to above, the Minister of Justice shall announce the naturalization by publishing the decree to that effect in the State Gazette.

7. In case the oath or promise of allegiance is not made within three months after the issue of the decree of the Minister of Justice, the decree shall automatically become void.

8. The amount of money referred to in paragraph 2 shall be refunded, if the application for naturalization is not allowed.

9. In case an application for naturalization is refused, the applicant shall be permitted to lodge a second application.

Section 6

With the approval of the House of Representatives, the Government can also grant naturalization on the ground of serving the interests of the State or on the ground of meritoriousness towards the State.

In such a case only the provisions of paras 1, 5, 6 and 7 of section 5 shall apply.

Section 7

1. An alien woman married to a citizen of the Republic of Indonesia shall acquire Republic of Indonesia citizenship if and when she makes a statement to that effect within one year after the conclusion of the marriage, unless she is still in possession of another citizenship at the time when she acquires the Republic of

Indonesia citizenship. In the latter case she shall not be permitted to make the statement.

2. Subject to the exception referred to in para 1, an alien woman married to a Republic of Indonesia citizen shall also acquire Republic of Indonesia citizenship in one year after the conclusion of the marriage in case within that year her husband does not make a statement to abjure his Republic of Indonesia citizenship.

Such a statement can only be made, and shall only result in the loss of the Republic of Indonesia citizenship, in case such loss does not render the husband devoid of any citizenship.

3. No other statement shall be permitted to be made in case either statement referred to in para 1 or 2 above has been made.

4. Such statement shall be made to the District Court or the Republic of Indonesia Representative Office in the town where the person concerned resides.

Section 8

1. A Republic of Indonesia citizen of the female sex who is married to an alien shall lose her Republic of Indonesia citizenship if and when she makes a statement to that effect within one year after the conclusion of her marriage, unless the loss of the Republic of Indonesia citizenship should render her devoid of any citizenship.

2. The statement referred to in para 1 shall be made to the District Court or the Republic of Indonesia Representative Office in the town where the person concerned resides.

Section 9

1. The Republic of Indonesia citizenship acquired by a husband shall automatically apply to his wife, unless the wife is still in possession of another citizenship upon the acquirement of the afore-mentioned Republic of Indonesia citizenship.

2. The loss of Republic of Indonesia citizenship by a husband shall automatically apply to his wife, unless such loss should deprive the wife of any citizenship.

Section 10

1. A married woman shall not be permitted to make the application referred to in sections 3 and 4.
2. The loss of the Republic of Indonesia citizenship by a wife shall automatically apply to her husband, unless such loss shall deprive the husband of any citizenship.

Section 11

1. A person who because, or in consequence, of marriage has lost his/her Republic of Indonesia citizenship shall recover that citizenship if and when the person concerned makes a statement to that effect after the dissolution of the marriage. Such statement shall be made to the District Court or the Republic of Indonesia Representative Office in the town where the person concerned resides, within one year after the dissolution of the marriage.
2. The provision of para 1 shall not apply in case the person concerned is still in possession of another citizenship after the recovery of the Republic of Indonesia citizenship.

Section 12

1. A woman who because, or in consequence, of her marriage has acquired Republic of Indonesia citizenship shall lose that citizenship if and when she makes a statement to that effect after the dissolution of the marriage. Such statement shall be made to the District Court or the Republic of Indonesia Representative Office in the town where the person concerned resides, within one year after the dissolution of the marriage.
2. The provision of para 1 shall not apply in case the loss of the Republic of Indonesia citizenship shall deprive the person concerned of any citizenship.

Section 13

1. An unmarried person under 18 years of age, who had legal family relations with his/her father before the father acquired Republic of Indonesia citizenship shall also acquire the Republic of Indonesia citizenship after he resides and stays in Indonesia. The statement concerning residence and stay in Indonesia shall not apply to a child

in case its father's acquirement of Republic of Indonesia citizenship should deprive it of any citizenship.

2. The Republic of Indonesia citizenship acquired by a mother shall also apply to her unmarried children under 18 years of age, who have no legal family relations with their father, upon their residence and stay in Indonesia.

In case the Republic of Indonesia citizenship is acquired through naturalization by a mother who has become widowed by the decease of her husband, the unmarried children under 18 years of age who had legal family relations with the afore-mentioned husband shall also acquire Republic of Indonesia citizenship upon their residence and stay in Indonesia. The statement concerning residence and stay in Indonesia shall not apply to children in case their mother's acquirement of Republic of Indonesia citizenship should deprive them of any citizenship.

Section 14

1. Upon attaining twenty-one years of age the child referred to in sections 2 and 13 shall lose its Republic of Indonesia citizenship if and when they make a statement to that effect. Such statement shall be made to the District Court or the Republic of Indonesia Representative Office in the town where it resides, within one year after the attainment of twenty-one years of age.
2. The provision of para 1 shall not apply in case the loss of its Republic of Indonesia citizenship shall render it devoid of any citizenship.

Section 15

1. The loss of Republic of Indonesia citizenship by a father shall also apply to the unmarried children under 18 years of age who have legal family relations with him, unless such loss shall render the children devoid of any citizenship.
2. The loss of Republic of Indonesia citizenship by a mother shall also apply to her children who have no legal family relations with the father, unless such loss shall render the children devoid of any citizenship.
3. In case a mother has lost her Republic of Indonesia citizenship because of naturalization abroad, and in case she has become widowed through the decease of the husband the provision of para 2 shall also apply to

the children who have legal family relations with the husband, upon their residence and stay abroad.

Section 16

1. A child that has lost its Republic of Indonesia citizenship because of the loss of such citizenship by its father or mother, shall recover the Republic of Indonesia citizenship upon attaining eighteen years of age, if and when he makes a statement to that effect. Such statement shall be made to the District Court or the Republic of Indonesia Representative Office in the town where it resides, within one year after its having attained eighteen years of age.
2. The provision of para 1 shall not apply in case the child is still in possession of another citizenship upon acquiring the Republic of Indonesia citizenship.

Section 17

The Republic of Indonesia citizenship shall be lost:

a. Upon the acquirement of another citizenship by a person's own will, on the understanding that in case the person concerned is in the territory of the Republic of Indonesia upon acquiring the other citizenship, his Republic of Indonesia citizenship shall not be considered lost until the Minister of Justice, with the approval of the Council of Ministers, declare the loss of such Republic of Indonesia citizenship, either of the Minister's own volition or at the request of the person concerned.

b. In case the person concerned, when afforded the opportunity, does neither abjure nor reject another citizenship;

c. In case an unmarried person under 18 years of age is acknowledged as a child by an alien, unless the loss of the Republic of Indonesia citizenship should deprive the person concerned of any citizenship.

d. In case a child is legally adopted by an alien before it has attained five years of age, and if the loss of the Republic of Indonesia citizenship shall not render it devoid of any citizenship;

e. In case a person at his request shall be declared to have lost his citizenship by the Minister of Justice with the approval of the Council of Ministers, if the person concerned has attained 21 years of age, resides abroad and has not been rendered devoid of any citizenship by the loss of his Republic of Indonesia citizenship.

f. In case a person enters the service of a foreign armed force without prior consent of the Minister of Justice;

g. In case a person, without prior consent of the Minister of Justice, enters the service of a foreign country or an international organization of which the Republic of Indonesia is no member, if, under the enactments and provisions of the Republic of Indonesia, such office in the service of a country can only be held by a citizen of that country, or if the holding of such office in the service of the international organization requires an oath or promise of office;

h. In case a person swears or promises allegiance to a foreign country, or part thereof;

i. In case a person, without being required to do so, takes part in the election of anything related to the political affairs of a foreign country;

j. In case a person is in possession of a valid foreign passport, or document having the character of a passport, written out in his name;

k. In case a person, for other reasons than the public service, resides abroad for five consecutive years, without stating his wish to retain his Republic of Indonesia citizenship before the expiry of the above mentioned five-year period, and afterwards before the expiry of every two years. Such wish shall be made known to the Republic of Indonesia Representative Office in his town or residence. For a Republic of Indonesia citizen under eighteen years of age, the afore-mentioned five-year and two-year periods shall not apply until he has attained eighteen years of age, unless he is or has been married.

Section 18

A person who has lost his Republic of Indonesia citizenship under section 17, item k. shall recover his Republic of Indonesia citizenship in case he resides in Indonesia by virtue of an Entry Permit and makes a statement to that effect. Such statement shall be made to the District Court of his town of residence, within the first year of his residence in Indonesia.

Section 19

A Republic of Indonesia citizenship granted or acquired on the ground of false statements can be revoked by the office that has granted the citizenship or by the office that has received such statements.

Section 20

A person not in possession of Republic of Indonesia citizenship is an alien.

TRANSITORY PROVISIONS

Section I

A woman who under section 3 of the Military Authority Ordinance No. Prt/ PM/09/1957 and section 3 of the Central War Authority Ordinance No. Prt/ Peperpu/014/1958 has been treated as a Republic of Indonesia citizen shall become a Republic of Indonesia citizen unless she is in possession of another citizenship.

Section II

A person who upon the commencement of the present Act is in the position referred to in section 7 or section 8, can make the statement referred to in the afore mentioned sections within one year after the commencement of the present Act, with the proviso that the husband of a woman has become a Republic of Indonesia citizen under the provision of section I of the Transitory Provisions shall not be permitted to make again the statement referred to in section 7 para 2.

Section III

A woman who under the laws operative before the commencement of the present Act would automatically be a Republic of Indonesia citizen if she were not married shall acquire Republic of Indonesia citizenship if and when she makes a statement to that effect to the District Court or the Republic of Indonesia Representative Office in her town of residence, within one year after the dissolution of her marriage or within one year after the commencement of the present Act.

Section IV

A person who has not acquired Republic of Indonesia citizenship together with his/her father or mother by the making of a statement under the laws operative before commencement of the present Act because such person was a major at the time when his/her father or mother made the afore mentioned statement, while such person was not allowed to make a statement to the effect of choosing the Republic of Indonesia citizenship shall be a Republic of Indonesia citizen in case he/she is not in possession of another citizenship under this provision or previously. The Republic of Indonesia citizenship acquired by such person shall be retroactive to the time when his/her father or mother acquired the Republic of Indonesia citizenship.

Section V

Deviating from the provisions of section 4 paras 1 and 2 the opportunity is afforded to children whose parents rejected for them the Republic of Indonesia citizenship in the period December 27. 1949 – December 27. 1951, to apply for Republic of Indonesia citizenship to the Minister of Justice through the intermediary of the District Court in the town where he resides, within one year after the present Act becomes operative, in case he is under 28 years of age; for the rest section 4 paras 3 and 4 shall apply.

Section VI

An alien who before the commencement of the present Act served in the armed forces of the Republic of Indonesia and meets the conditions to be laid down by the Minister of Defence shall acquire Republic of Indonesia citizenship in case he makes a statement to that effect to the Minister of Defence or to the official appointed thereto by the Minister of Defence. The Republic of Indonesia citizenship acquired by such person shall be retroactive to the time when he entered the service of the Republic of Indonesia armed forces.

Section VII

A person who before the commencement of the present Act serves in a foreign armed force as referred to in section 17 item f. or who is in the service of a foreign country or an international organization as referred to in section 17 item g. can apply for the consent of the Minister of Justice within one year after the commencement of the present Act.

FINAL PROVISIONS

Section I
A Republic of Indonesia citizen who is in the territory of the Republic of Indonesia is considered to possess no other citizenship.

Section II
The term citizenship includes all kinds of protection by a state.

Section III
For the purposes of the present Act, an unmarried person under eighteen years of age shall be considered to reside with his/her father or mother under the specifications referred to in section 1, items a, b, c and d.

Section IV
Anyone who is in need of evidence that he is a Republic of Indonesia citizen and who cannot produce documents in proof of the fact that he possesses, has acquired, or shares in the possession or acquirement of the afore mentioned citizenship, can apply to the District Court in the town where he resides, for a decision whether or not he is a Republic of Indonesia citizen under the ordinary civil procedure.

This provision shall not prejudice the extraordinary provisions referred to in, or based on, other laws.

Section V
The official concerned shall submit copies of the statements causing the acquirement or loss of Republic of Indonesia citizenship, to the Minister of Justice.

Section VI
The Minister of Justice shall announce the names of the persons who have acquired or lost their Republic of Indonesia citizenship, in the State Gazette.

Section VII
Any matter required for the implementation of the provisions of the present Act shall be regulated by Government Ordinance.

Section VIII
The present Act shall come into effect on the day of promulgation, with the proviso that the provisions of section 1, items b to j. section 2. section 17, items a, c and h. shall be retroactive to December 27. 1949.

In order that everyone can take cognizance, this Act shall be promulgated by publishing same in the Republic of Indonesia Gazette.

Sanctioned in Djakarta,
on the 29th day of July, 1958,
The President of the Republic of Indonesia,

SOEKARNO

The Minister of Justice,

G. A. MAENGKOM

Promulgated
on August 1. 1958.
The Minister of Justice,
/s/ G. A. MAENGKOM.

STATE GAZETTE No. 113 OF THE YEAR 1958.

AGREEMENT ON THE ISSUE OF DUAL NATIONALITY BETWEE THE REPUBLIC OF INDONESIA AND THE PEOPLE'S REPUBLIC OF CHINA*

(Translation)

The Government of the Republic of Indonesia and the Government of the People's Republic of China, on the basis of the principles of equality, of mutual benefit, and of non-interference in domestic policies of each other's country; desirous of settling in the best possible way and through friendly cooperation the dual nationality of persons who have at the same time the citizenship of the Republic of Indonesia and of the People's Republic of China, decide to enter into this agreement and have for this purpose appointed their plenipotentiaries:

> The Government of the Republic of Indonesia:
> H. E. SUNARIO,
> Foreign Minister;
> and
> The Government of the People's Republic of China:
> H. E. CHOU EN-LAI,
> Foreign Minister,

who, after having communicated to each other their full powers and found them in good and due form, agree to the following provisions:

Article I
The contracting parties agree that anybody who at the same time has the citizenship of the Republic of Indonesia and of the People's Republic of China shall choose between the two citizenships on the basis of his or her own will.

A married woman with a dual nationality shall also choose one of the two citizenships, on the basis of the will of the person concerned.

Article II
Anybody having dual nationality as mentioned under Article I who is already of age at the time this agreement comes into force shall choose one of the two citizenships in two years' time after ratification presumably.

Persons considered of age under this agreement are those who are fully eighteen years of age, or those who are not yet fully eighteen but already married.

Article III
Anybody with dual nationality as mentioned under Article I who wishes to retain his or her Indonesian citizenship shall state his or her desire to abandon the citizenship of the People's Republic of China to the officers of the Republic of Indonesia in charge. After having expressed this desire the person is considered to have chosen the citizenship of the Republic of Indonesia on his or her own will.

Anybody with dual nationality as mentioned under Article I who desires to retain the citizenship of the People's Republic of China shall state his or her desire to abandon Indonesian citizenship to the officer of the People's Republic of China in charge. After having stated this desire the person is considered to have chosen the citizenship of the People's Republic of China on his or her own will.

Officers of the Republic of Indonesia in charge are in the Republic of Indonesia officers appointed by the Government of the Republic of Indonesia; in the People's Republic of China the Embassy of the Republic of Indonesia and the Consulates of the Republic of Indonesia in the People's Republic of China – if they exist – and temporary offices which on the basis of their being needed are established by the Embassy or Consulates concerned and staffed by their officers. For the establishment of the temporary offices the agreement of the Government of the People's Republic of China shall be obtained.

Officers of the People's Republic of China in charge are in the People's Republic of China officers appointed by the Government of the People's Republic of China in the Republic of Indonesia, the Embassy of the People's Republic of China and the Consulates of the People's Republic of

China in the Republic of Indonesia, and temporary offices which on the basis of their being needed are established by the Embassy or Consulates concerned and staffed by their officers. For the establishment of the temporary offices the agreement of the Government of the Republic of Indonesia shall be obtained. To enable persons with dual nationality to choose their citizenship the two contracting parties promise to agree to a simple expression of the desire.

Provisions for choosing the citizenship laid down under this Article basically also apply to persons with dual nationality as mentioned under Article I residing outside the territory of the Republic of Indonesia and the People's Republic of China.

Article IV

The two contracting parties agree that anybody with dual nationality as mentioned under Article I who has chosen the citizenship of the Republic of Indonesia according to the provisions of this agreement shall automatically lose the citizenship of the People's Republic of China, and that anybody with dual nationality as mentioned under Article I who has chosen the citizenship of the People's Republic of China according to the provisions of this agreement shall automatically lose the citizenship of the Republic of Indonesia.

Article V

The two contracting parties hereby agree that anybody with dual nationality as mentioned under Article I who does not express the choice of citizenship within two years as stipulated under Article II shall be considered to have chosen the citizenship of the Republic of Indonesia when his or her father's side is of Indonesian descent, and shall be considered to have chosen the citizenship of the People's Republic of China when his or her father's side is of Chinese descent.

When the person concerned has no legal relation with his or her father or when the father's citizenship is unknown, the person shall be considered to have chosen the citizenship of the Republic of Indonesia when his or her mother from the father's side is of Indonesian descent, and the person shall be considered to have chosen the citizenship of the People's Republic of China when his or her mother from the father's side is of Chinese descent.

Article VI

Anybody with dual nationality as mentioned under Article I who is not yet of age at the time the agreement comes into force shall choose his or her citizenship within one year after coming to age.

While still under age, the person concerned shall be considered to have the citizenship of his or her parents' choice or of his or her father's choice according to the provisions of this agreement.

When the person concerned has no legal relation with his or her father or when his or her father has died before declaring his choice of citizenship within the stipulated period or when his or her father's citizenship is unknown, the person shall be considered to have the citizenship of his or her mother's choice according to the provisions of this agreement.

Article VII

Anybody with dual nationality as mentioned under Article I who has adopted the citizenship of the Republic of Indonesia and has lost the citizenship of the People's Republic of China, shall automatically lose his or her citizenship of the Republic of Indonesia when such a person, after leaving the territory of the Republic of Indonesia, has established permanent residence outside the territory of the Republic of Indonesia and has regained the citizenship of the People's Republic of China on his or her own will.

Anybody with dual nationality as stipulated under Article I who has adopted the citizenship of the People's Republic of China and has lost his or her citizenship of the Republic of Indonesia, shall automatically lose his or her citizenship of the People's Republic of China when the person, after leaving the territory of the People's Republic of China, has established permanent residence outside the territory of the People's Republic of China and has regained the citizenship of the Republic of Indonesia on his or her own will.

Article VIII

Children born within the territory of the People's Republic of China possess the citizenship of the Republic of Indonesia as from the dates of their births when their parents or only their father possess the citizenship of the Republic of Indonesia.

Children born within the territory of the Republic of Indonesia possess the citizenship of the People's Republic of China as from the dates of their, births when their parents or only their father possess the citizenship of the People's Republic of China.

Article IX
A child, citizen of the People's Republic of China, legally adopted by a citizen of the Republic of Indonesia while still under five years of age, shall by virtue of this be considered a citizen of the Republic of Indonesia and shall lose his citizenship of the People's Republic of China.

A child, citizen of the Republic of Indonesia, legally adopted by a citizen of the People's Republic of China while still under five years of age shall by virtue of this be considered a citizen of the People's Republic of China and shall lose his citizenship of the Republic of Indonesia.

Article X
When a citizen of the Republic of Indonesia marries a citizen of the People's Republic of China, each respectively shall retain his or her citizenship before the marriage unless one of them by his or her own will applies and obtains citizenship of the other. When he or she obtains the citizenship of the other, automatically he or she shall lose his or her original citizenship.

Application for citizenship as mentioned above shall be made to the legal authorities of the country concerned.

Article XI
The two contracting parties agree in the interest of the welfare of their respective citizens residing in the country of the other contracting party, to urge the party's respective citizens residing in the country of the other contracting party, namely, the citizens of the Republic of Indonesia residing in the territory of the People's Republic of China and the citizens of the People's Republic of China residing in the territory of the Republic of Indonesia, to abide by the laws and customs of the State in which they reside and not to participate in political activities of the country in which they reside.

The two contracting parties agree to give mutual protection according to the laws of the respective country, to the legal rights and interests of the respective citizens residing in the country of each contracting party.

Article XII

The two contracting parties agree that exchange of mind between the two parties shall be made regarding questions of implementation which are not provided in this agreement.

Article XIII

The two contracting parties agree that any disagreement arising out of the interpretation and implementation of the agreement shall be settled through negotiation between the two contracting parties.

Article XIV

This agreement shall be ratified by the two contracting parties in accordance with their respective constitutions and shall come into force as from the day of exchange of the instruments of ratification which shall take place in Peking.

This agreement shall be in force for the duration of twenty years and shall continue to be in force unless one of the contracting parties desires to annul it. Such desire shall be notified in writing to the other contracting party, following which the agreement shall expire within one year after the notification is made.

IN WITNESS WHEREOF the plenipotentiaries have signed this agreement and have affixed thereto their respective seals.

Done in duplicate in Bandung, on April 22nd, 1955, in the Indonesian and Chinese languages, both texts being equally valid.

For the Republic of Indonesia,   For the People's Republic of China,

/s/ Sunario   /s/ Chou En-lai
Foreign Minister   Foreign Minister

SPEECHES DELIVERED AT THE SIGNING OF THE TREATY OF DUAL NATIONALITY BETWEEN THE REPUBLIC OF INDONESIA AND THE PEOPLE'S REPUBLIC OF CHINA.*

Dr. Sunario, Foreign Minister, Republic of Indonesia:

Your Excellency, the Foreign Minister of the People's Republic of China,

May I first, in the name of my Government of the Republic of Indonesia, express happiness at the fact that agreement has been reached between our Government and Your Excellency's Government as regards a settlement of the question of dual nationality between our two States. The reaching of agreement is clear from the signing of the text of the Treaty just now.

The signing of this Treaty is an event of the greatest importance not only for our State and People but also f0r the State and People of Your Excellency.

For is it not true that this Treaty opens up the possibility of putting an end to a situation which has gone on for years and years, but which we now regard as no longer fitting?

Our Government is happy too because this signing has come at the very time of the holding of the Asian-African Conference, which is also an event of historic importance in the relations between the States of Asia and Africa.

Everything can go smoothly when an atmosphere of neighborliness prevails, which it is to be hoped will always prevail between the State of the Republic of Indonesia and the State of the People's Republic of China.

Thank you.

---

* Text as given in *Asian-African Conference: Speeches and Communiques*, Ministry of Information. Republic of Indonesia (Mimeo. , Djakarta, May, 1955).

Mr. Chou En-lai, Foreign Minister, People's Republic of China:

Your Excellency our respected Minister for Foreign Affairs Dr. Sunario, Gentlemen,

It is a great privilege for me to sign today on behalf of the People's Republic of China "The Treaty between the People's Republic of China and the Republic of Indonesia concerning the question of Dual Nationality. Allow me to extend on behalf of the Government of the People's Republic of China our sincere congratulations to the Government of the Republic of Indonesia and to Your Excellency Foreign Minister Sunario.

The Republic of Indonesia and our country have always maintained good neighborly relations. Our two countries have always respected and have been friendly to each other. The question of dual nationality is a question left to us by the past. Now it is reasonably settled through friendly negotiations between the People's Republic of China and the Republic of Indonesia in accordance with the principles of equality, mutual benefit and mutual respect.

We know that some other countries are likewise concerned about this question. It is of great significance that this question is solved during the time of the Asian-African Conference. This is another good example of solving difficult questions between us Asian and African countries in a spirit of friendly negotiation.

I guarantee that the Government of the People's Republic of China will firmly carry out the Treaty signed today. I hope that persons of Chinese origin with dual nationality as a result of past history will, after making their choice of nationality in accordance with their own will, strictly abide by the letter and spirit of this Treaty and increase their sense of responsibility towards the country the nationality of which they have chosen. I hope that persons who choose either the nationality of the People's Republic of China or the nationality of the Republic of Indonesia will join their efforts in promoting friendly and neighborly relations between the People's Republic of China and the Republic of Indonesia.

I congratulate the ever strengthening of the friendly relations between the People's Republic of China and the Republic of Indonesia!

APPENDIX EIGHT
SUMMARY OF GOVERNMENT REGULATION NO. 20. 1959. CONCERNING THE IMPLEMENTATION OF THE DUAL CITIZENSHIP TREATY BETWEEN INDONESIA AND CHINA*

Article I

1. Rejection of Chinese citizenship must be made at the District Court in one's place of residence in Indonesia, or at an Indonesian consulate or embassy if one is overseas.

2. Rejection of Chinese citizenship may be oral or written. There will be no tax or fee. Oral rejection will be on a specified day. If too many people come to Court on that day, they will be registered and will be invited to return later to complete arrangements.

3. (This section lists the various forms, documents, and procedures required for written renunciations)

4. If the court official who receives a renunciation believes that it is not allowable, the letter of renunciation may be returned with reasons for its rejection. Letters of renunciation may also be returned for correction or addition of omitted information. A person whose renunciation is rejected will have four months in which to prove his right to renounce Chinese citizenship.

5.-7. (Procedural technicalities)

8. A person's certified copy of his letter of renunciation becomes his proof of citizenship. "This certificate loses force as proof of citizenship if it is declared invalid by the Minister of Justice or a judge of a District Court."

---

* This regulation was dated May 26, 1959, and made law on June 1, 1959, but it did not come into effect until January 20, 1960. The present summary is based upon the text as reported in *Pos Indonesia*, July 15. 1959.

9.   The Minister of Justice will declare a registration as invalid if the person concerned did not have the right to reject Chinese citizenship.

10.-11. (Procedural technicalities)

Article II

12. Those who will be considered already to have rejected their Chinese citizenship (and hence will be exempt from the option requirement) are as follows:

   a.   persons who have already sworn allegiance to Indonesia as a member of some official body
   b.   members of the Armed Forces, or those honorably discharged therefrom
   c.   members of the Police Forces, or those honorably discharged therefrom
   d.   veterans
   e.   civil servants and civil servant pensioners
   f.   civil servants of autonomous areas and pensioners
   g.   persons who have more than once represented the Government of Indonesia in the political field, and who afterwards have never represented the Government of China.
   h.   persons who have more than once represented the Government of Indonesia in the field of economics, and who afterwards have never represented the Government of China.
   i.   persons who have more than once represented Indonesia in the field of culture or of sports in international competition, and who afterwards have not represented China.
   j.   farmers whose way of life and relations with native Indonesian people demonstrate that they are natives themselves, in the opinion of the Ministers of Home Affairs, Justice, and Agriculture.

No one will be considered to fall into any of the above categories who has shown disloyalty to Indonesia.

13.   Also not included among non-opters are women who at the time the treaty comes into effect are married, and children who at the time the treaty comes into effect are minors, *if* the husband or father or

mother whose citizenship they follow has dual citizenship but does not fall into any of the categories listed above.

14. Wives and children of those who are considered to have already given up Chinese citizenship automatically acquire Indonesian citizenship also.

15. As soon as possible after the treaty comes into effect, lists will be made of those who are considered to have given up Chinese citizenship. The lists will be drawn up by the following officials for the respective categories listed above:

   a. the heads of official bodies
   b. the Minister of Defense
   c. the Head of State Police
   d. the Minister of Veterans Affairs
   e. the respective Ministers
   f. the Heads of Autonomous Areas
   g. the Minister of Foreign Affairs
   h. the Minister of Economic and Industrial Affairs
   i. the Minister of Education, Teaching, and Culture
   j. the Minister of Home Affairs

16. The Minister of Justice will be given a copy of this list.

17. Those listed will receive certificates of Indonesian citizenship.

18. Those listed as having lost their Chinese citizenship may regain it and give up Indonesian citizenship by so stating within one year. This also applies to those mentioned in (14).

19.-22. (Procedural technicalities)

Article III

A prison sentence of one year and/or a 100, 000 rupiah fine is provided for not returning a certificate when asked, or for giving false information.

INDEX

This book is indexed using Google Book Search.
Kindly visit books.google.com and enter in the title or ISBN.

www.ingramcontent.com/pod-product-compliance
Lightning Source LLC
Chambersburg PA
CBHW020001290326
41935CB00007B/262